WHEN THE DANDELIONS SING

By

James J Hill III

ISBN paperback-978-1-7367105-0-0

ISBN hardback-978-1-7367105-1-7

Copyright James J Hill III

Also available on ebook

Contact the author at:

jamesjhill3rd@mail.com

JamesHillAuthor.com

Facebook.com/JamesHillWriter/

Instagram @girldadof5

Dedicated to my Mother and Father,
and my five beautiful girls
Taylor, Sophia, Sadie Grace, Scarlett, and Stella

A special thanks to my dear friend Cat, for all the help in the editing process.

CONTENTS

"Dear self,"

No. That just makes no sense at all. Writing a letter to my much older self should not start off as "Dear self," although, well, I am writing to myself, technically. Kind of seems strange to refer to me by my name, though, so maybe "Dear self" works? Maybe I can just write it and use my given name.

"Dear Ronnie."

Should I use my full name or is that too much? I do not want my older self to think I was a dweeb for writing out my full birth name, Ronnie Jefferson McFarland Jr. That would seem as if I were trying to sound too grown up, and although I am for my current age, that may be pushing my intelligence a little. Not even I would believe it when I read it, to be honest. Was I important enough to get away with that?

I could use my Grammy's nickname for me. Jasper. It means nothing, really. At least, I don't think it does anyway, but when I was a baby, she told my momma I did not look much like a Ronnie to her. She was actually dumbfounded that Momma had named me Ronnie, and not Ronald, or Donald, or something that Ronnie would derive from. No, she just called me Ronnie, which brings about another curious issue. How was I Ronnie Jefferson McFarland Jr if my daddy's name, as far as I knew anyway, was not even Ronnie Sr.? So, Grammy told my momma she was not going to be calling her grandson a name that made no sense to her at all. Nope, I looked like a

Jasper to her, so she would call me Jasper, and that was that.

I liked Jasper. It was kind of a funny name, but still, it did have a certain ring to it. When Grammy would call us in to eat, she would just scream for my brother and sisters by their own names, and then last, but not least, she would scream, "Jasper! Get in here. Supper's almost ready!" None of my siblings had a special name like that. They had dumb names like David and Janet and Thelma Louise. Nope, not me. I was not ever going to be Ronnie to her. I was Jasper, and that was perfectly fine by me. It set me apart because I was clearly Grammy's favorite. She would not tell me that, but we all knew.

Davey teased me about it all the time, telling me Jasper meant that Grammy thought I was stupid, or that because I did not have a "real" first name like they did, that she made that one up because she figured any foolish name would do. He said she just found it while she was in town one day and some guys were teasing each other, calling themselves Jaspers. I knew better, though. Grammy, even when hollering at us all for whatever dumb thing we had done, would wink at me afterward, when the others were too busy getting upset or washing up. She never admitted to it, though. I asked her once about that and she told me I was acting a fool, that she had not winked, not ever. Not even once. I felt like maybe I had imagined the winking incidents, but the next time we got in trouble for coming in late, all muddy and tracking dirt in the house and onto her gleaming, freshly mopped hardwood flooring, she winked again. She did not smile when she did, though. She just winked, showing the long lines around her eye, and looked away. I knew she did that because I was her Jasper. I was certainly different from the others. The youngest of all the grandkids, and I had the strangest first name to her. So, she took a different liking to me for sure. I just knew it.

Back to my pending letter, though. This is harder than I anticipated. I am trying to write a letter to my much older, hopefully, more mature self, because I want to remember the events unfolding here and now. This would be a moment in my life I surely would need to document, so I would never forget it, and I did not even know how to address myself in the letter. If you cannot address yourself properly in a letter, you simply cannot write the letter. Otherwise, it is just a letter to basically anyone. What if I forgot I wrote this letter, and my future older self, found it and forgot who wrote it and why? Maybe I would just crumple it up in my hands, throw it away in a wastebasket and not read it at all, because there was no name to start it off. It was a major problem I had before me for sure. A big dilemma for me, so I asked Davey for advice.

"Hey, Davey, how do you write a letter to yourself without sounding all stupid and such?"

"You don't," Davey replied quickly. "Who writes a letter to themselves, anyway? That makes literally no sense at all. I mean, you are right here. Just tell yourself what you need to tell, yourself," as he chuckled at me with his response in jest.

"Oh, and what did I tell you! It is not Davey. It is David. I am not like you at all, having a stupid first name that isn't even formal. That's not even normal. I have a formal first name. It is David. D A V I D. Say it, David."

Momma always said Davey was mad when I was born. He

had been the baby of the family, and having two older sisters, he felt he had it made in the shade. He could do whatever he wanted because the sisters loved playing with him like he was a real-life doll baby of theirs. I would laugh and tell Momma he still looked and acted like a doll baby, and she would tell me to knock it off with her smile and say, "A little he does, doesn't he?" She knew I was kidding, but it was all I had to get Davey back with. He was exceedingly stronger than me, a great deal smarter than me, and well, he did not like me much. I wanted to play with him all the time, but he just did not see the fun in doing that. He had his friends, and they always ran as fast as they could when I would try to tag along behind. I kept trying, figuring one day my legs would just magically shift faster back and forth, just fast enough to catch them, and they would be surprised and let me play just because of that. It never happened though, despite my trying over and over. I did not want to give up until they let me play. I was determined. But the faster I got, the faster they seemed to get.

"Okay, Davey, I'm sorry. I just wanted to know, you know, how you would write a letter to someone, like if you had to write one to yourself for school, how would you start it off? That's all I was asking," I said, not wanting to sound foolish.

Davey looked at me, with the slight grin he always looked at me with, tied his tie around his neck as properly as he could, and rolled his eyes upwards into the back of his head, and shook it. He would not be of any help, I could clearly see, so I needed to ask someone else. Maybe Janet would be able to help me better. She was smart, 15 years old, and she liked me even though we were 7 years different in age and had literally nothing in common. She was a quiet, slender figured girl with long, straight, dirty blonde hair that fell naturally to the floor, and it was always neat, sometimes tightly braided in the back, but never on the sides.

Janet was in her bedroom, which was at the top of the stairs, where there once had been an old dusty attic. Grammy and Grandad had turned that dark space into a bedroom when we all moved in. The room had low curved ceilings on the outsides because the roof was there just on top, but you certainly could walk down the middle, and on each side were daybeds—one for Janet and the other for Thelma Louise. Janet always had to have the left side. She was the only one of us who was left-handed, and she favored anything to that side for some odd reason. She always felt the need to sit on the left side of the car, she ate on the left side of the booth in Roxy's Diner when we went into town on Sundays for Church, and she would always pick something up from the ground below her, from her left side. Even if she had to turn completely around, she would pick things up with her left hand only, but people didn't really say much to her about it, because it was causing no harm, as Momma told me, and she would eventually just outgrow it, she figured.

"Janet, can you help me with this, please? I want to write a letter to myself, well, my older self to be exact, and I do not know how to address myself, my older self. How would you address you if you were writing a letter to your older self so that you knew when you read it later, it was from you, to you?"

Janet looked at me, made a short-drawn smile, and shook her head, as if to say, what on earth are you talking about,

Ronnie, but it was not to be mean at all. She really tried to understand me as best she could with the age difference and all, and I always tried to explain things to her the best I could, but I was only 8 so it did not always come out right. Plus, I talked super-fast when I was excited and felt the need to get it out right away. Sometimes even quicker than my mouth could get the words out, and I stumbled over them, so my thoughts were all jumbled as they left my lips. I wanted to just get everything out before I forgot it, so I tried my best to do just that. She knew that and would always tell me to slow down some. To take a deep breath. That I would remember the important parts, and that would be enough. She was right, but they were ALL important parts to me. I genuinely had a lot to say, but now I just needed an answer to my letter problem so I could continue with the meat of the letter. I had not even written any words at all, because I had no idea how to start it.

"Ronnie, just start it by saying, dear Ronnie. That way, you will know it is meant for you, and you will be using your name, which I have never met another Ronnie. No one will confuse you with, well, you. You do not need to write out your full name. Where are you going to put the letter anyway?" she asked.

I had not even thought about that. Where would I put this letter so that no one would get to it before I did? Plus, it had to be in a spot that no one would find it for a long time. I wanted to make sure I only read this when I was old enough to understand, and who knew when that would be. Plus, I had to remember that I wrote the letter in the first place. That was another perplexing problem altogether. How could

I open it and read it if I did not even remember where I had hidden it years before? It had created more problems asking a simple, basic question, and now I was getting frustrated all over again. It was already a sad day, but I was trying to be strong and just get things together in time and write this one letter to myself before we left.

The letter would just need to wait. It was time to get going, and the car was pulling up and outside now, waiting for us. The ride was not a short one, so I had plenty of time to think about the letter and how to address it perfectly. Plus, I now needed to find a place to hide the letter, where no one would find it, but myself when I was old enough to understand. The trip would provide me with plenty of time, I thought. I could figure this out, and then when we were done, come back home and sit back down at the dining table, and write my letter out. I had to go now, so that would just need to wait a little bit longer.

Chapter 1

The Birth of Ronnie

* * *

Because of the rapidly accumulating snow laying softly on the roads in town, Momma had to be particularly careful driving herself to the emergency room after her water broke while carrying me. She was working at Roxy's Diner part-time, while going to school to learn how to do important office work, or something like that. She said she needed to educate herself on how to file important time-sensitive petitions (whatever those are), how to talk with people on the phone who were always demanding and screaming, and how to handle others in suits who had come from better backgrounds than any of us had. She knew that if she worked hard enough and was dedicated to what it was she wanted to do, we could all grow up to wear suits one day too and be just as important as those folks were.

Momma was always working towards something better. A way to get all her kids dressed well for their jobs, so she could in time look back on her hard work and know all those long hours of studying and working late, was for good reason. She did not want the same old same old over and over anymore. She wanted to break the recurring chain, she said, and give us a better chance at life. Plus, she figured at least one of her kids would succeed enough to take care of her, when she grew old, frail, and tired and needed to retire. She was always talking about retiring. I had no idea what any of that meant, but I knew I wanted to give her that one day. I would be the one making all the money, telling people what to do and they would have to listen to me, and Momma would be so proud of me, as she sat, retired, drinking lemonade on her front porch. I do not know what else she would be doing while retiring, but I wanted to do that for her because it is what she wanted.

The time was not right for my arrival though. She was only 34 weeks pregnant and I was coming before she had a chance to prepare all the other children at home. When she left that afternoon, just after her classes finished for the day, she figured she had a few more weeks left in her to work the diner, and finish out her semester at school, with plenty of time to have me and then get back to class and work. I was not having it, as Grammy would say. When I wanted something, I was persistent. This was just the start of my persistence, apparently. The world was a big, beautiful place, full of curious wonders, attractive dancing colors bouncing around, and riveting sounds. These were things I just had to know about. So, I was being my impatient self, and broke Momma's water so I could come out and see all the things I needed to.

Because the diner was packed, being that it was supper time, and guys and girls were just finishing work at the nearby steel plant, Stapleton Brothers Steel Works, Momma told her boss she would just drive herself. This was her fourth baby, and she was fine enough to know she had plenty of time to get to the county hospital on the other side of town, have me, and be home by the following evening, resting in bed. Besides, they were short-staffed as it was.

The snow was falling hard, and the other waitresses did not have four-wheel drive, so getting in was not a problem, but getting home would be an entirely different story. Momma had a faded Orange Scout with a white stripe a third of the way up, so she could get around just about anywhere she needed to. The driver side door would stick more often than not, so she would need to either crawl through the window or open the passenger side and crawl across the seat, over the center console, and into the driver seat. It was winter, so the driver side window was naturally up already. This made it so she would need to open the passenger side door, pull herself up to the seat, slide across the hard, freezing, cracked black leather, over the center console, and pull her body under the steering wheel so she could start the Scout and drive.

Momma loved her orange and white Scout, but it had grown temperamental. She'd had the car ever since Grandad gave it to her and it was getting old. She hated asking for things, but more so, she hated that her kids would go without if she did not. Momma was always putting her pride aside when she really needed to, and Grandad never

3

made her feel bad about it. He knew she was struggling and trying with good intent, and just having some dumb bad luck, but he blamed himself for not giving her the life he had envisioned for her years before. This was why he was proud of her. She was going to school, something he had never done. Nor had anyone in his family he could remember off hand. She would be the first, and he was proud of that fact. She would break that link in the chain and change paths for her kids. That made him pleased to help her whenever he could, and so he did.

As soon as she was under her steering wheel, strapping the seat belt over her shoulder and stomach carefully, and she had pulled her keys from her purse, she said a quick prayer. She needed the Scout to give her no trouble. Just do its job and start, get her to the county hospital, and then it could do whatever it wanted. She just needed this to go smoothly, so she sat there, eyes closed and hands woven tightly together, prayed there, and placed the keys in the ignition. Then she gave it a turn. At first, it seemed like her prayers had fallen on deaf ears as the Scout just cranked and cranked, but she did not give up hope, and finally, it turned over and started. She put her head gently against the steering wheel, and whispered to either God or her car, "Thank you. Thank you…Thank you."

Momma put the Scout in drive, cleared off the front windows with the wipers as best she could, and pulled out of the parking lot in front of the diner. She drove past the neon sign missing the Y forever, it seemed, so people called the diner "Rox's," and onto the white snow-covered road.

As she went right, she realized the hospital was only about a ten-minute drive, and that she would easily make it if nothing happened along the way. Things were looking up, and she needed this desperately. It was time for a change, and this would start her off onto a new, greater path.

Momma had had some bad luck in the past that always seemed to surface at the wrong time, but she never let that get her down for long. She always told me that if butterflies could come from a wormlike creature, turn into a hard shell, become a pile of mush and guts inside that shell, and then emerge this gorgeous, beautiful, colorful creature, then God could do the same for her. She was, after all, just like a butterfly. She had been a scrawny kid growing up, much like a worm is, and she had learned to grow a hard outer shell because she was picked on so much as a child, plus she was full of guts and mushy things, I figured, and eventually, she would emerge into a beautiful creature, although I always saw her as pretty anyway. She was just tough on herself. Grandad said she was always looking for more in life than she had so she would be hard on herself until she had it. He never felt she would ever get enough, though, and he admired that. She was always yearning for more. She would read books on everything and anything, always keeping her mind sharp as a tac, and work hard at the classes she attended. She would fall asleep at the dining room table on many a night and wake up just in time to get us kids ready for school, then go back to class herself, then to the diner, and home to repeat it all over again. Day after day, and night after long night.

By the time she pulled up to the county hospital parking lot, the snow was slowing some to a soft drizzle, and she could see through the night much better. The brilliant white snow had created a glow on the road, and as her lights danced back and forth off the cresting snow, she was singing to herself a song to keep calm. She was making the words up, trying to stay in tune with the lights dancing on the road, and trying to pass the time as quickly as she could. I was coming, and she knew I would not wait much longer. She needed only to get to the front doors, and they would quickly bring her a wheelchair out, and she would be in their hands, thank God. She kept telling herself it was just a few minutes away. The entire time she told herself that, even though the snow made it an arduous journey more than it would normally be. Her song kept her feeling comfortable and surprisingly calm, and she sang and sang, impressing herself with the words and the tune she carried, that seemed to just come out of her mouth in a poetic, rhythmic way.

When she finally pulled up, parked, and turned off the Scout, she was putting her keys in her purse and getting ready to exit through the passenger side when she felt a sharp pain in her abdomen. She hunched over instantly, holding her right side tight with both her hands, and breathed rapidly. As she tried to slow it down, the pain grew more and more intense. She would wait it out, she thought, and then continue with her crawling to the other side of the car so she could pull herself down and into the waiting hospital only a few dozen yards in front of her.

She just needed to be patient and calm, and she tried her best to be just that.

To distract herself Momma sang again, through the searing pain, and this time the words did not come as easily as they had earlier. She tried to remember the song she had just made up that had been beautiful and flowing and came so easy to mind, but she was now struggling to form even one line. Maybe if she just tried to focus on her breathing, how she had done with each of her other three kids, she would be just fine. So, she counted her breathing, how long the breaks between the sharp dagger in her side were, and noticed they seemed to be getting shorter and shorter. Growing more concerned, her last thought was to lay on her horn, and pray someone inside would hear her Scout's cry for help, come out and help her. This would be harder than she anticipated, and she was now getting quite nervous. Never one to be nervous for the most part, she scared herself. Panic was taking over, and she knew she had to do something, anything, and fast.

It was getting late, and the heavy snow now covered all the spots next to where she parked. Because she was feeling pretty good on the way over, she had not pulled up to the entryway, and now she was regretting that decision. Momma was a strong-minded person, always out to prove her worth, and she wanted to walk in by herself, just as she had driven on her own, with no help from anyone. This was her trip, her journey, and she was tired of people telling her how to travel it. She would be damned if she let anyone tell her she could not, when she knew clearly, she could indeed. But this? This was scary. This was not normal, and she was willing to let others assist her only when she was at her end, and she was getting pretty damn close.

As she leaned forward, still clutching her stomach with her right hand only now, feeling like lightning was striking her abdomen over and over, she laid on the horn, and for dear life, she pushed as hard as she could with her free left hand. The air was quiet, and it was probably heard for a mile away, but no one came. She started to cry, now hitting the horn in repetitive motions, hoping someone inside would tire of the racket, and come out to see what was going on in their parking lot. So, she hit it again and again, and through her tears, the sheer pain, and the slowing snow, she saw not a soul. That is when Momma gave it all she had and fell onto that horn with both her hands and her head, and with all her might. Knowing she was about to pass out from the pain, yet not willing to let that noise stop until someone, anyone, heard it, and helped.

That was all she remembered of that night. She collapsed onto the hard black steering wheel and fainted from the increasing nonstop pain. In her mind, no one heard her at all, and no one would come to her aid. Her greatest fear that evening was that she would not be able to keep her weight on the horn while she was unconscious, and no one would find her and her baby until the next morning, and this hurt her more than the pain she felt in her abdomen.

Within minutes of her passing out, a nurse working behind the desk, stepped outside for a cigarette break and looked out into the parking lot. She heard the steady noise of the horn coming from this snow-covered, faded orange Scout, and quickly ran back inside to get security to check it out. When they arrived at the car, they noticed Momma was passed out at the wheel but did not know that she was pregnant just yet.

The dark cover of night made it hard to determine what was going on exactly, and they could not pry the driver side door open, figuring it was simply locked. One guard walked around to the passenger side and discovered that it was unlocked. When he wiped the snow off the handle, opened the door, and gently pulled her head off the steering wheel to stop the obnoxious noise, he quickly told his partner and the other nurse that had walked up with them, "This lady here is pregnant!" They worked to get Momma out, and after realizing the driver door was busted and would not open, they slid her over, carefully, to the open passenger side. One of the guards picked her up in his arms, turned to the nurse and asked her to check on her, and they realized she was alive. He hurriedly carried her through the slippery parking lot, being so careful not to slip on the slick snow covering everything in sight, and into the front doors of the emergency room.

The front desk nurse ran to fetch a wheelchair, and they placed her in the chair as gently as they could and pushed her through the second set of doors, into an open area where doctors and nurses were talking about this and that, and to a room just off the hall. He laid her down on the bed, helped the nurse remove her jacket, and watched as she seemed to just sleep through it all.

Having done all he could, the guard backed up, just into the hall but not out of sight. He could see and hear the doctor, now checking her vital signs, and shouting orders to the nurses that had also clambered into the room to see what was happening with this woman. The floor-length white curtain around her bed were closed hastily, and the old security guard, who had eight grandchildren of his own, leaned against a wall and mumbled a prayer for the young delicate-looking woman he had just carried through the dense snow, to get her the help she so desperately needed.

By morning, Momma had made it through, and she had a second son to show for all that pain. When she came around, she realized what had transpired the night before and smiled gently, knowing that once again, when she had a desire to do something, she did it regardless of the odds stacked against her. She knew that laying on that obnoxious horn had saved her life and the life of her baby, and it took everything she had in her to do that simple mindless task, yet she had done it. Not knowing how the night had gone was somewhat of a relief to her. Her side had stopped the sharp, piercing pain she felt just the night before, and for that she was relieved. She noticed the snow outside was falling once more, and the fresh coat of white made her feel at peace.

My Grammy and Grandad came to the hospital as soon as the storm allowed, and Momma noticed that her dad looked exhausted. He had not been feeling himself, and when he heard from another waitress that she had driven herself through the snowstorm to the emergency room, he was sick to his stomach. Momma was his only daughter, and he wanted things to turn around for her desperately. It was just his way, to want his children to have all they could ever dream of, but his drive was not as strong as it had once been.

He had fallen victim to a job that, while paying the bills and providing for him and Grammy in their retirement years, was far short of what he had intended when he was a young man. He had hopes, dreams, and goals to pursue. He was strong, hardworking, and although not properly educated, had the mind to fix anything around him that could be broken. He was a gentle giant, and how his large frame had produced such a frail, tiny, almost fairy-sized woman, was anyone's guess. Maybe that was why he tried to do so much for Momma. Because she was so different, so small, so fragile. You would never know it, though, because Momma was a pistol. She allowed no one to get over on her. People knew who her daddy was, and they feared what he could do with those massive hands of his, but she had been determined to have people respect her just the same, and they eventually did.

"Hey, little DeeBee, how are you feeling?" he said to Momma.

Momma was born Dolores Grace McFarland. But Grandad called her "DeeBee," because she was tiny, but had the bite of a buzzing bumblebee at the end of the summer, knowing it was about to end its life cycle. From an early age, she had that bite. No one else could call her by this nickname but her daddy because he had made that up for her, and it was their thing. At 5' and ¾" tall, you would think people wouldn't care much for what she preferred, but she was respected. People did not go out of their way to bother Momma. Maybe Grandad had something to do with that, maybe not. Either way, it did not matter. She was respected from the time she was in high school and stopped taking bull from anyone and everyone around her. People liked her, but they also respected her for her passion towards life.

"I'm feeling fine, Daddy, only tired and woozy. What did they give me this morning? I cannot feel what they did to me at all. I feel like I am on a floating cloud looking down and watching this all happen right here and now!"

"You are just fine," he said smiling. "The doctors know what they are doing. You just rest now and let us take care of the kids. Besides, you haven't even told us what you named your boy yet. What's our newest grandson's name going to be?"

All at once, Momma felt very confused, and as if she were not even in the room. Somehow, she was holding onto me, bundled neatly in a blue, pink, and white striped blanket, and had not even known if or what she had named me.

"Nurse, Nurse!" she called out.

"Yes, dear, what is it?" the nurse replied.

"I am sorry, I feel so out of it, and I just realized I have not given you the name of my baby yet. When do I give you that?"

The nurse smiled at Momma, and simply told her,

"Dear, you named him first thing this morning. You

were adamant, in fact. Don't you remember that at all?"

Embarrassed now, Momma did not know what to say. She did not know much about my father at all. He had told her so many lies while eating in the diner, that she thought she knew, but quickly realized she did not. Now, her baby had a name she knew nothing about and had no recollection of it coming from her lips.

Grandad quickly interjected,

"Miss, she's had a long night. I am sure you understand. Would you mind telling her mom and me the name? I know she wanted to surprise us, but now that the secret is out, we just would like to know the full name, just the same."

"Oh, of course. I am so sorry. She named the baby, Ronnie Jefferson McFarland Jr."

That is how I entered this world, on a blistering cold, snowy February morning. Ronnie Jefferson McFarland Jr, although my father was, as far as we all know, not named Ronnie Jefferson McFarland Sr. That part simply remained a mystery, and I was ok with that. I had my momma and she had me. All was good with our world.

Chapter 2

A Legend

* * *

Grandad had been born in the same exact town we now live in, Red Creek, Pennsylvania, in the same area we are staying in now to be exact. 1701 Old Spruce Drive was our address. In the summer of 1918, there was a pandemic known as the Spanish Flu, and it was causing a crazy mess throughout the entire world. Sadly, it did not miss the old dusty country town of Red Creek. Families were completely wiped out, decimated, and people's lives were changed forever. Grandad told me once that his Momma had been really sick while carrying him, and that she had gone to God just after he was brought into this new world. I asked him why God had taken her, and not someone else's momma and he would just say that lots of Momma's had gone together. That maybe God decided he needed the best ones up there to take care of all those little kids that were going home as well. It was a tough time, and Grandad did not remember too much about that all, except for the stories his own daddy told to him. Or maybe he just did not like to think back on them.

"Do you miss your momma?" I asked.

Grandad would look at me with his warm brown eyes, and somehow, he understood my curiosity was not meant to pry or to open old wounds, but to understand better. He would gently pick me up with his massive strong hands, place me on his lap and tell me the stories of how he had grown up, and no matter how often he told me the story, I listened intently. Each time I felt I learned something different or heard a distinct word I did not hear the last time or saw a different look of emotion on Grandad's face. Sometimes he would look as if he were thinking back to that olden time, and his expression would be one of getting lost in the story he was narrating, while others, he would be more interested in my expressions and reactions to what he said.

Grandad was the type of man who always took his time to explain things with great detail, because he knew the smallest details were more important to me than the actual story was. He enjoyed that about me. I would sit on his lap and just stare at him as he told his stories, and I would imagine myself as someone in each of his tales. When he talked about the time he was born, I would think back to when my momma had me, and how she told me she almost did not make it through that day. What if she had not made it through? What if I had come into this world on that cold February night, and she had died? Would I be sad still? Was my grandad sad that his Momma left him, or had he always been brave? I did not know, but still, I always listened.

By the time I was a little boy, Grandad was graying. Not just his hair either, but his skin too. He was strong, but he was feeling the effects of growing up as he had, working whatever jobs he could find until the steel plant had come calling. His hair was thinning and receding a little more each year, and his smile caused his face to exhibit more crevices than it had the story before.

As he'd tell me stories, I'd study the lines on his face, deep like the paths carved into the mountain by the water near Potters trail, just north of our home. We hiked there and Grandad told me about adventures he and the "boys" took running through the caverns and splashing in the crick down below the valley. We never understood why other boys in different towns called it a creek. Creeks were bigger. This was in fact, a crick. Those were, as he told it, the best times of his youth and he thought of them often.

His hands were powerful from moving heavy steel around for decades, and they showed dark brown spots and soaked blue veins that were hard to miss. He was tall but now slightly hunched over, seemingly not the great giant he once was. All in all, he was still imposing, if only because of the stories people told about him. I was unsure if they were more legend than reality, but he was my grandad and when I was out with him, I felt 10 feet tall. I walked with my head higher, and my chest puffed out a bit more. Everyone went out of their way to greet him, and subsequently me. I was always proud to be his sidekick on our trips into town.

When Grandad's mother passed, his Auntie Clara Dell

moved in to help take care of things around the house. She had no children of her own and had never been married either. She was a plump, loud character, as Grandad explained her to me while smirking. She was always smiling and laughing emphatically, even when nothing was particularly funny. She found good and humor in just about everything around her. It was not that she had not wanted to get married and have children of her own, she just did not ever get around to it. For years she taught school in the next town over, and those students felt like her own. She would read every evening after supper, and never found much time to find a suitor. He told me she was a happy person, though, regardless, and figured she had bigger things to do, and enjoyed giving to others. So, naturally when her brother came calling for help, she found purpose and knew it was what she was intended for. It was a natural progression for her, even though she had no children of her own. Her brother needed her, and she would need no time to think things over. She sold her one-bedroom home, packed just enough of what she would need to, and moved across the town border, into Red Creek, and settled in.

Grammy was not from Pennsylvania. She was never supposed to be here at all. She was born Mildred Elizabeth Hale down south, just outside of a town now known as Peachtree City, Georgia, on a family farm that sold tobacco to larger farms. She had it rough, and her parents had divorced early on, leaving her Momma with her and her 6 siblings, alone. Grammy moved to Pennsylvania when her own Momma met a man traveling through the State of Georgia on his way to Ohio in search of work by the waterways of Lake Erie.

They quickly connected and fell in love, leading them to travel north together, with all the kids in tow, to a new life in an area foreign to them both. They would need to pack light, and trust that each would help the other through the transition. They put everything they had in their faith in each other and hoped for the best. When they stopped over in Pennsylvania on their plotted-out course, one of Grammy's brothers came down with tuberculosis and could not go on further. He fell sick quickly and had to rest. They found a small shanty to rent temporarily, and her new husband found local work to provide supper for the family and to pay the rent, until they could finish their journey. Years passed, and they never made it to Ohio. Life would start over for them in Red Creek, and they would make this home for good, as best they could.

Grammy and Grandad met at a small general store on the corner of Haw and Blue Ridge roads. Grandad drove me by there once and showed me where it had been. Instead of the store he fondly remembered, there stood a larger store with bright blue and white lights, and the uneven, dirt sidewalks had been replaced with solid, smooth concrete. The once quiet area was bustling with cars and people all about. I had known no different, but Grandad seemed to be let down a bit. He missed the way it had been, the way his life was vastly simpler, and the energy he once had.

I think Grandad felt he could have done so much more with his time, and that he had let life pass by him without realizing it. Often, I would see him stop his old rusting red chevy pickup, look over to a spot where something new was in place of something old, and talk about what once stood there proudly many years before. His eyes would get fixed on what seemed like nothing, and he would gaze and just sit forward, peeking through the dirty windshield to what was in front of him. I would ask him what he was looking at, but he was not listening by that point. He was in a different time, a different era that had long since passed him by, but he was still there. He had an ability to get lost and reminisce about what he once had, and how he would give just about anything to go back to that lost time in his life. In those moments, it was as if he was back there, living in that olden time, searching for something he once held so dear to his heart.

They married in the summer of 1936, when Grammy was just a 17-year-old girl. They moved to a second-floor apartment building, over top of Red Creeks Country Store and Supplies, the same general store that they met in several years prior. Grandad was working as a carpenter with his uncle, but then a friend of his, John B. Rogers, had told him he could get him a job working next to him at the steel plant. Because of his broad shoulders and natural big stature, he would be a shoo-in for sure. They would likely hire him on the spot, and that is exactly how that happened. He was hired immediately and started his new life as a steelworker for Stapleton Bros. Steel Works. Meanwhile, Grammy was at home, tending to their tiny but cozy one-bedroom apartment, honing her cooking skills, and trying to provide a nice place for Grandad to come home to after the long days in the steel plant.

When Grammy had her first child, a boy, Grandad had just shy of a full year under his belt at the plant, so money was still extremely tight. He looked for extra hours, trying to get noticed for his hard work ethic, and eventually, he secured more overtime. This caused a dilemma at home, though, because Grammy did not get to see her new husband much during the week at all, and she would sit with her newborn son William and dream of the days when Grandad earned enough to come home at a reasonable hour for supper like so many of the other husbands could do.

Grandad was a tough, hardworking man, and although he felt his wife's anguish for certain, he knew he needed to work hard if he wanted to be successful in life and give their family a better chance to get ahead. Being raised by his Aunt had taught him a lot of valuable lessons, one of which was to chase after dreams a little bit harder because time would not slow down just because you needed it to or wanted it to. No sir, time would simply feel as if it were passing by faster and faster, until you were old enough to have raised children of your own, retire, and while smoking a tobacco pipe on the front covered porch of the home you had worked hard to pay off, look back with pride at all you'd accomplished. Grandad dreamt of this, and of grandkids playing in the front yard while he rocked and puffed away on his pipe, his wife by his side and a pitcher of iced lemonade on the table. That was certainly a different ending than the one he'd actually created, but time had just simply gotten away from him while he was busy chasing after his goals.

When the Great War arrived and Pearl Harbor was attacked surprisingly, many young men saw a different future than the one they'd planned. They saw one where their freedom was threatened. One where tyrants ruled over them with an iron fist, telling them how to act and what to do. That did not sit well with them. They were hard-working countrymen with values and morals, and when the time came to fight, fighting is exactly what they did. Proudly, they enlisted one after the other, without a moment's hesitation.

Grandad was among those who joined the Army, and during the Spring of 1942, he was headed overseas to fight in a war that meant more to everyone back home than it did at any other time in history. That is how he saw it anyway. The "Japs" had invaded our home soil, threatened the families we loved, our freedoms and our way of life. "They were not going to take that without a good ol' country boy fight," he said. During one firefight, Grandad had a shell go off close enough that the dirt covered his body up to his neck, keeping him from being able to dig himself out, and panic set in. Two men from his platoon quickly came to help him, and despite the constant barrage of fire flinging by like lightning bugs illuminating a wheat field, they dug him out, and Grandad continued the fight. He was a tough ol' backwoods country boy, as Grammy would say. "You could not keep that man down for nothing," she told us.

When the Great War ended, a smaller number of boys

returned to Red Creek than had gone over. The little town had lost a great deal of its boys, and women quickly became widows. Pride had meant little to these families without fathers. Children, some who had never even met their daddies, had no way of understanding what happened. For Grammy, she was just happy that her husband had returned as he promised he would in one piece. He was a little different, though. A little more tense, a little more unaware of the family, and a little more restless.

Grandad's job at the steel plant was waiting for him when he came home, and he worked long hours again. After work was finished for the day, he would stop on the way home for a beer with the boys and talk about the war, the steel plant, the weather. Then one beer would turn to two, and two to three. Eventually, Grammy would need to take his wallet, remove all his cash he had stuffed inside, and place it back in his pocket before he left in the morning for work. After a few times of embarrassment, she would relent and leave enough for a drink or two if he promised to come home right after. She knew he was dealing with something she could not understand, but she was as well. It was her responsibility to take care of the house, clean up, cook the food, tend to the kids, wash the clothes, and pay the bills. She was wearing thin, and their relationship was suffering deeply.

One night, Grandad stayed out a little longer than expected, and Grammy was worried more than usual. He had been good and honored his one to two drink promise he made her, so she did not think he was out drinking more. She could not leave because she now had 3 children at home and was pregnant with number four. So, she went down the hall, over to where Mrs. Talbot lived and asked if her husband would mind walking the four blocks to the bar to retrieve her husband and bring him back on home. Mrs. Talbot knew the McFarlands well, and she knew they were decent folks.

"Honey, you just wait right here, and I'll fetch the Mister and have him run down straight away to see if we can rustle up old Walter for ya."

Walter, or Grandad, went by Walt, but Mrs. Talbot had a bad time remembering the names people preferred, and so he just never reminded her after a while. He would just have to be Walter to her, but no other person dared go against his wishes. He was just plain ol' Walt.

Mr. Talbot was a shorter, older man, slightly round and unassuming. His face was soft, and he wore tiny wire-rimmed glasses as he could not see more than 3 feet in front of him. He was a quiet man, allowing Mrs. Talbot to do most of the talking for them both, but he had a big soft heart.

Mr. Talbot put on his heavy navy-blue overcoat, wrapped a soft tan scarf around his neck, kissed Mrs. Talbot on her rosy cheek without even raising his eyes to meet hers, and set out into the dim hall, down the stairs, and out the door to the waiting street. As soon as he did, Mrs. Talbot told Grammy to hang tight, and she would throw a pot of oriental tea on so that by the time they were finished drinking it, ol' Walter and Mr. Talbot would be back on their way up the stairs, and all would be right again.

As they sat there sipping on hot tea, Grammy calmed down some, and she and Mrs. Talbot talked about the frigid cold, how the people of the town were adapting to the growing population boom, and how they were glad the war was over. Grammy was a smart, understanding woman, and she understood Grandad had a lot of trauma dancing around in his head from what he experienced while fighting in a land he knew nothing about, or had ever even heard of for that matter, before he deployed. He once told her he was not so worried about the boys that did not come home, as much as he was for the ones who had. Oh, he was sad at the loss and knew their families would suffer for a long time to come, missing and aching for the husbands, sons and fathers they lost. The boys who came back though had seen what he had seen, and for them their minds were not the same as when they had left. They viewed life and circumstances in a very different way now, a way haunted with the memories of what they had seen and done.

Once, when he was picking up some split apple wood for the fireplace, a man chopping more wood nearby inadvertently dropped the ax onto a metal plate causing a loud bang. Grandad hit the ground in a frantic manner, looking feverishly all around, and screamed for the other men to hit the deck as well. It was not until a few moments later that he realized where he was, and what was going on. The men said nothing because they just knew. Most had either been where Grandad was or knew someone close that had. Many had relatives and friends that had not returned at all.

It was an unspoken understanding, and when Grandad realized what he was doing, he got up, embarrassed, and confused, shook off the damp dirt from his shirt and jacket and walked over to the man. He paid him, never looking at him directly, and apologized. The man quickly said, "Walt, no need to say anything, friend. I did not see a thing. See you next week, big guy." That was enough to get Grandad through what he had just felt. That war had more lasting effects than anyone could have expected, including my big ol' Grandad.

Chapter 3

The Story

* * *

Chasing my brother Davey and his friends Maack and Howard was frustrating, but I was determined not to give up. Little by little, I would find ways to inch closer and closer to them as they glided down the street with their leather baseball mitts, wooden bats and a ball, heading towards the field to play ball until the sun went down. I would wait just up the road some and spring out when they got close enough, feeling as if one day, any day now, they would relent and just let me tag along.

"Jasper go home. You are too small to play with us, and besides, Grammy needs you to do your chores and keep her company," he said as he laughed with his buddies.

"Davey," I begged. "Come on, Davey, let me play! I can chase the balls you don't want to go after. The ones you hit real hard and that roll all the way into the brushy weeds. I can get those ones for you!"

Howard, well, Howie as my brother Davey called him, would always try a little for me.

"Davey, let him play. Come on, he can chase what we don't want to, and then we can have more time to hit and run. Let 'em tag along, Davey. You know you hit those dang weeds all the time."

"Stop calling me Davey for one, you know I hate that. Besides, you are only calling me that because my little brother is too dumb to remember my real name. Just because he has names that have no meaning whatsoever, doesn't mean I do. I was named after David Crosby. A singer I was named after. My mom picked my name because she liked it, not because she couldn't find a better one."

Sometimes I would win, and they would let me tag along. Most times, Davey would win, and I would not. The days I could follow them all the way to the field, I was made to carry the bats and mitts and the balls, while they ran side to side, singing and laughing all the way to the field. The bats would drop, and I would need to pick them up, only to have the mitts drop, and then the balls. At the field, I would try to run down those whizzing balls as fast as I could, throwing them back with all my might. It would take me two, sometimes three attempts to get the ball back to where they had been, but I would just keep running up, throw, run further, throw. What did I care? I was out in the warm summer sun, with Davey and his best pals, chasing dreams and pretending like I was one of them, or even better yet, a real ballplayer.

Life was good on those days. Even when Davey would throw the ball as hard as he could in the wrong direction, just to watch me run. He was trying to make it so I would not want to play more and just give up, but I did not care. I would drop my head and just run as fast as my legs would take me in the opposite direction, chasing down that heaved ball, picking it out of the overgrown weeds and thorny brush, and fling it back high into the air. Davey was watching me, and I felt that although he would never tell me, he was proud that I was not giving an inch.

Back at home, Janet and I would switch up doing the supper dishes. Mostly, though, she would wash, and I would dry. It was hard for me, being smaller, to reach the ones in the back of the sink, so Janet would just say "Don't tell Grammy we didn't switch, we can just keep this between us, Ronnie, okay?" She was always understanding and good to me. Maybe because she was older. Maybe because she and Davey did not always get along. Davey was always angry and storming off when he didn't feel much like talking. Janet was quiet, kind, just a good-natured person all around. She knew I struggled to play with Davey and his friends. She knew all I wanted to do was fit in with my brother and the boys. To feel like a part of a "club," or a group that had my back, and I would have theirs. She knew. That's why I liked her so much. She understood me, and she was always telling me that my day would come when it would be my turn to shine and stand alone. My turn to stand out from the crowd, and my turn to be in charge. I wanted to believe her, but that just seemed so far away. I wanted that here and now, but I knew she was right. Maybe anyway. I would just need a whole heaping lot of patience.

Thelma Louise was the oldest of us four, and therefore

she was not around much. When she was home, she was up in her room, or sneaking out the backdoor to go meet some boy she'd met at school or running off to just escape it all. She did not talk much to me, because she was so much older, and we had nothing really in common, but she was good still. She never yelled at me. She would ask me to sneak out one of Momma's cigarettes occasionally, and I would. Momma knew she had smoked before and scolded her good, but that didn't stop Thelma Louise. She just found better ways to hide it. She would keep a bottle of mouthwash in her purse, and gargle it before she came in. She would hide a change of clothes in the plywood shed out back and switch her outfit before she entered the house. Momma never caught that because she was too busy working and trying to get us back out on our own again. She had a good job, but she still had trouble making ends meet sometimes, even with Grammy helping any way she could.

I sat with Grammy one evening on the porch and asked her about my name. I told her that Davey was making fun of me because I had been named after no one in particular, and she would just tell me that Davey was going through a phase and he would come out of it just fine. She told me that other people's opinions of me were not my business and I should not worry myself about what people thought of me, or my name. Besides, how many people had Jr at the end of their name, even though they were not named for a particular person? I mean that was something to find special. To want to show off. It meant that I had something others did not. I was a junior, even though I was not.

Davey couldn't claim that. He was named after some singer Momma had never even met. I had four names. Ronnie Jefferson McFarland Jr.

Never had I thought of it like that, but she was on to something. I had more names than Davey. One of those names was a president. Maybe Ronnie was a different type of name, but it was mine. I was not Ronald. I was not Donald. They may have used Ronnie as a nickname, but I owned this name. I was Ronnie without having to shorten it. Plus, I was a junior, even though I had no idea what that meant. I still was, though.

"Jasper listen to Grammy. You should always be proud of who you are, and what your name is. It says a lot about you boy. I did not give nicknames to any of the other grandkids. Just you. You are my little Jasper, and that is a very good thing. Don't let Davey or any of those other neighborhood boys make you feel bad about that. Jasper is who you are to me, and I do not give out names lightly. Grandad knows you are a Jasper too. He just lets that be my name for you. It was and is very special to me, and he knows that. You may be Ronnie to him, but to me, Jasper it is. When you are 30, and mature and have a family of your very own, you will still be Jasper to me. Don't you ever forget that you hear" then she winked at me.

"I won't, Grammy. I won't."

Then I would ask questions, more questions, because I just always wanted to know everything. My mind worked in a different way than it did for Davey. He was only inter-ested in what was going on in the right now. How many strikeouts Nolan Ryan had thrown the night before, or who was playing the Reds that night? Knowing about his family, his life, what had happened before him that allowed him to be wherever he was at the moment, was not on his radar, but it was on mine. I wanted to know it all.

"Grammy tell me what happened to Grandad again, you know, back when you was married living in that apartment. Before you moved to this place. Tell me that story?"

I did not need to elaborate. Grammy knew the story I was referring to. She knew I had a curiosity for how Grandad had gotten in trouble, and how it turned his life around. How he had not come home that evening, or for a time to come, and how he somehow ended up here in this house, the very one we were sitting on the steps of. Grammy told the story a half dozen times, and I knew it well, but I liked the way she told it. She told me as if she knew I was all eyes on her, my ears opened fully and my heart pounding against my chest as she began.

"Oh, Jasper, the story. Well, sure. I will tell you the story, but then you need to go wash up and get ready for bed. You hear? We have a big day tomorrow."

I sat down on the rust-colored wood-planked porch, crossed my legs Indian style, and put my hands under my chin to hold it up, as I listened to Grammy tell it.

"Grandad was out having his one beer, the allowance I kept in his wallet for the day. He usually was able to get the bartender to give him another round, by arm wrestling some other big sap steelworker who had had many more beers than he. I guess their wives had yet to figure out my

31

little trick, but Grandad was never one to let someone stop him and how he was going to carry on. While he was walking home, he, for some reason or another, took a detour down Bachman's Alley, just beyond the southern edge of the steel plant. It was getting late, and maybe he just had to take a pee. Maybe he felt like something had pulled him in that direction. Whatever it was, he was now walking down the alley way, making a short detour before finishing his walk home. It was dark, and there was only one working streetlamp in the entire alleyway. Some local kids had used their BB rifles to shoot out the others, but this one hung much higher, and none had been able to knock it out just yet."

Grammy pulled her glass a little closer, took the pitcher of lemonade off the table, poured herself a tall glass, and sipped it, looking out to the street in front of the house. As she paused, I looked out to the road. It reminded me of Grandad looking at an empty lot that had once been a marvelous building, where some family he knew had lived, or he had treated some gal he met to ice cream. That look I remembered well, and I always looked with them, hoping to catch a glimpse of what they had seen.

After a few moments, she continued but still had her eyes on the road in front of her.

"Well, anyway, Grandad was walking down the alley when he heard a ruckus going on, just about 20 yards away, on the opposite side of the steel plant where he was employed, and he went over to investigate. He was slowly approaching, aware that the freshly snow-covered ground had created black ice under his feet, but also that he had no idea of what exactly he was about to run into. Plus, only he knew for sure how many beers he had consumed earlier that day. When he was close enough, he peeked through the thin brush hiding the yard from view and saw 3 silhouettes prying the basement doors to what could have been an abandoned house," Grammy paused as though trying to remember the story the exact way Grandad told it.

"As he told me later, he was going to just walk on and let it be for the cops to handle, but something in his gut pushed him on still. He leaned over the fence, just enough to be in view, and shouted to the figures to get the hell out of there. Instantly they stopped and turned, facing where Grandad had been, and began to look at one another, hoping that one of them would know what to do. The houses were all oddly attached, and so there was only one way out, and that was where Grandad had been, just on the other side of the fence there. They quickly grabbed the tools they were using, and without taking their eyes off Grandad, began to walk his way. Now Grandad had no way of knowing if these people were going to simply walk on by him, or perhaps come at him aggressively, or if they had maybe owned the place and were simply trying to get in because maybe they had lost the keys."

She took another break, sat back in her chair, looked this time down at the decking of the front porch as if she were wondering if she should stain them again or wait another year, and took another long sip on her glass of lemonade she had in her hands still.

"Well, as luck would have it, it was three boys from a neighboring town. They had been searching for vacant homes that were easy to break into, hoping to remove the copper pipes for scrap I suppose, and whatever else they could find. Grandad had a sense for things like this and was usually right. This time he was dead on. When they got to where he was leaning just over the broken picket fence, two quickly jumped and hightailed it down the snow-covered alley, but one was having trouble. Grandad, by this point, figured he would just help the boy over and let them be on their way, just stupid kids making stupid decisions he had thought, and began to reach over to grab the boy and lift him the rest of the way over. The boy must've got nervous, and when he saw Grandad's hands close, he hit him with a piece of jagged steel he had in one of his hands. Grandad was cut from one side of his palm, clear to the other and started to bleed real bad. His instinct, combined with the beers he had consumed that evening, caused him to lash aggressively at the boy. He grabbed harder this time, calling the boy a dang fool, and pulled him up and over the fence in one motion. The boy slipped, tumbled over downward, and hit his head on the snow that was covering the hard gravel alleyway. It was not what he had intended to do to this boy at all, but sometimes what we intend to do is not what happens at all. No, sometimes greater, rougher, more heartbreaking things happen in life than what we intend. This, this was just one of those types of moments."

Grandad had more than a few beers that night and was saucy to those around him. That was the word Grammy used, saucy. She had meant that he was drunk, angry, and confused. He had not intended to hurt anyone that night. Only to take a little longer walk to possibly sober up some, knowing he was not supposed to be drinking as he had that night.

The boy, named Frederick Johnson, was 13 years old, and although Grandad screamed for help to come, no one had heard. A lot of that street had been vacant for some time. People did not want to live right alongside the steel plant any longer if they could help it, so they moved further out when possible. Most had already departed the area, and only a few remained. They, however, either did not hear Grandad's roaring screams for help or did not want to get involved. So, Grandad picked this small boy up, this Frederick boy, and carried him over his shoulders, all the way down the dimly lit alley, and over to where the old hospital had been.

When he arrived, he laid the boy down on the cold waiting room floor, looked at him, and cried out, "What have I done?"

Frederick died late that night, and Grandad was promptly arrested. He did not fight. He did not argue. He just went with the officers. The wound to his hand, blood-soaked clothes, and the fact the boy had a large gash on the top of his head from the sudden fall, led the police to believe they had a fight, and this big man, this oversized drunk steelworker, had gotten the better of this frail 13-year-old boy. It did not look good for Grandad, and he did not protest. He was ashamed and could not collect his thoughts well enough to put together what had really happened. His life had changed in an instant and he would now always be linked to this horrible tragedy, and the boy's family would be altered forever. He was not coming home, and for the time being, neither was Grandad.

Chapter 4

The Cufflinks

* * *

Y ou ever just meet someone and know instantly that they are genuinely special? Well, that was my momma. Just watching her, you could tell she was something else for sure. Raising us four kids mostly by herself, while working several jobs at a time, going to school, and trying to keep her head above water, was all she knew how to do. After her scare with me the night I was born, Momma said she made it a solemn promise to not have any more kids. Grammy didn't believe her, but Momma said she was positive she was done this time. She was finished and if that meant she would not have another man in her life, well, then that is what it meant. She had high hopes for us four, even Davey, who was mean to me, but whatever. She loved us all the same. We all loved her, too. She was tired when she would come home from work, but she always made time for each of us as best she could. It wasn't that she had a huge amount of energy, but what energy she did, she spent on us.

By the time she finished her business schooling, Momma did not need her waitressing job anymore. Instead, she worked in a fancy firm where all the guys wore black suits, pushing papers from one side of the desk to the other, in a 2-story brick building that had lots of windows, in the center of town. She spent her time making folders with all different color tabs on them for the suits to pick up and look over. She envisioned us all wearing them suits one day, and nodding our heads, saying something like, "yes, good work. These look splendid. Have these completed by five pm and leave them on my desk."

Momma was always dreaming for us because we were dreaming about baseball and being astronauts and stuff like that. Well, Davey and I, anyhow. My sisters thought of other things, like boys. They were always thinking about boys. I have no clue why. Besides, I did not want to ever wear a suit. Ties bothered me. They were tight around my neck, and always made me itch, and besides, they were ugly. I didn't understand why anyone would want to wear a tie. What was the point? They were just stupid anyway, but Momma said that a man in a tie was usually someone important. That he had earned that tie, and because of that, he had every right to wear it as he pleased, even if it did not feel good on his neck. Well, if I became an important person, I would not be wearing a tie. I would start a trend. No one would wear ties. As a boss, I would send people home if they wore a tie into the office. It would be my first rule. No ties allowed, or else.

One day, Grandad came over to me and handed me a box.

"What's in it?" I asked, confused.

"Open it, Jasper. Grammy and I thought this was a nice gift to you. A just because type of gift, for you."

So, I opened it up, and inside were two round dull silver bead type things. I hadn't the faintest idea of what they were, but I still said thanks anyway and made a smile as if I knew.

"Jasper, you know what these are? These are cufflinks. Sterling silver cufflinks. A man a long time ago gave these to me and he told me that one day these would look fine with a suit and tie, but I never had a shirt that would take these," he said.

"Well, what do you do with them?" I asked, confused.

"You wear them, of course, Jasper. You put them on a shirt that has slits in the sleeves. When you wear a fancy suit one day, you be sure to get a shirt that accepts these, and you wear them. You will look sharp as a tack with these on, son. Sharper than a tack, in fact."

Grandad sat back, smiled widely and you could tell he was proud of this moment. I still had no idea of what to do with these dull metal silvery things in the box. After all, I owned no jewelry at all. I didn't even own a suit or a tie yet. I doubted that I ever would if I had anything to do with it. I know Momma wanted this for me, and now it looked like Grandad was on board with her, but me? No sir. This boy would not be a tie-wearing suit looking type of man ever. The only suit I wanted to wear was pinstripes. Baseball players wore uniforms and to me, that was cooler than any old suit you could buy in the fancy stores. They were important men, and they did not need a suit to play. Grownups were so strange. Why wear something that was tight, and uncomfortable anyway? Maybe I just wouldn't grow up. How about that I thought to myself.

He told me to put cufflinks in a safe place for safekeeping, and so I took them to my room, opened the brown shoebox I had with all my favorite baseball cards in it, moved them carefully out of the way, and dropped the cufflinks to the bottom of the box. I then placed the cards back in the box, covering the small black square velvet box they had come in. This was the safest place I could think of because I treasured my baseball card collection. More than anything I owned I treasured them.

Momma would let me buy one pack of those baseball cards each time I would do all my chores properly for a week straight. I did not miss one time. I wanted those cards. They kept me occupied. Opening the wax-lined wrappers, smelling the bubble gum before I even got to the cards themselves, I slowly savored that moment. You do not know what heaven is like, until you smell the back of a pack of cards, sealed in wax, with bubble gum inside. At least, that is how I saw it. It was just the best smell. Even better than bacon in the morning. Although, that is a pretty good smell too. The wax would have just a slight resistance, and then you would peel it back slowly, softly, unaware of what cards were to follow. Were you going to pull out an all-star card? That one player you could just not find, like he was avoiding you altogether.

I loved baseball and I had my favorite players. I wanted

that Mark McGuire rookie card. Or that Eric Davis card. He was my all-time favorite. We did not live in Cincinnati, but he played for the Cincinnati Reds and I liked him best. He was the type of player who could do anything, and he hit the ball incredibly hard. When I played ball with Davey, well, when he actually let me, I would pretend I was Eric Davis, and run the ball down, losing my hat to the wind on purpose, and throw it like a slingshot into the air. My arm would come all the way back to the ground, almost touching the tips of the blades of grass below, and as soon as it slung up, I would release the ball. It never went far, but it did not matter. I was still Eric Davis. It did not even matter he was black, and I was white. I was five and so none of that mattered none to me.

The cufflinks were stored away, and I forgot about them. I had no reason to remember them now, so off I went to play in the rear yard, digging up worms and building fortresses out of rocks and sticks I had gathered from my walks with Grandad, when we hiked down at Potters Trail. Each time I did this, Davey would come out and kick them over.

"Why are you building dumb stuff for stupid worms? You should be saving the worms for fishing, not building them houses to live in," Davey would tease, and then walk away, out of sight.

I would just pick the worms back up from where they landed and start all over again. I didn't care that Davey did this. It was more the worms I was concerned about, but they did not seem to mind none. They would crawl around the rough rocks, over top of the broken sticks, and onto my soft hands. I would sit there for hours watching them, wondering if they communicated with each other and how they did. Wondering if they were thankful for the home I had just built them, that protected them from the large black crows high above.

I camouflaged them with thick crabgrass so that from the sky, they would blend into the rear yard, but down here below, they were palaces, like the houses on Bridge Street, that ran through town. Those houses were ginormous. I once bet Davey that a king must live in one of those, and his princes and princesses lived in the others. He would laugh and tell me I was stupid for thinking such nonsense.

"No way a king lives in there. Listen here, we don't even have kings here. We have Presidents. Kings live somewhere far away, like in the orient some place. These houses? These are owned by some old gray-haired men who happened to strike it rich somehow. Probably from the steel mill. That is who owns those houses. Not some made-up kings and princes and princesses."

Davey sounded smart, but I still did not believe him. I meant to ask Grandad but kept forgetting with all I had going on. I bet he would know, though. He would know who owned those grand houses. He probably had met the men and women who lived there, to be honest. Everyone knew Grandad and everyone liked him. I am sure of it. He would know and I would ask, but first, I had to finish protecting my slimy friends, the worms, from those ugly black crows. I did not like crows. They made funny noises while circling high above in the clouds, and always scared me when they stared in my direction. They were just big, ugly, stupid birds anyhow. They wanted my worms, and they could not have them.

I was the worm protector. Yea. The worm protector. King of the worms. The worms would love me and know I was safe, and they would enjoy their new homes and always want to come back when I was out in the yard. These worms I would not use for fishing. These worms Davey could not have. No sir, these were my worms. The worm protector's worms.

When Davey was about to come into the world, his dad left Momma alone in the hospital to have him. He just dropped her off at the entrance, told her he would park the car, and well, that was that. He never parked the car, at least not there anyhow. Momma knew something was wrong, and had been for a while, but she did not expect to be abandoned at that moment. Her labor was long and strenuous, and after she realized he was not coming back, she was stuck with breathing those deep in and out breaths all alone, through the sharp pains of a difficult labor, and wondering what she would be going home to when she finally got out. She was a fiercely strong woman, but being there, not having anyone to help, and helpless to the fact that he was taking whatever he wanted and leaving, she was crushed. I think she was too embarrassed to call Grandad and Grammy. They had told her for years they did not like her husband Andy.

Andy was a drifter of sorts but held semi steady jobs in and around the town. She had told him that Grandad could get him a job at the steel plant if he desired, but Andy always felt he knew better. He did not want a handout as he saw it, and always had big plans. Big plans, that went nowhere. That was how Grandad saw him. Always dreaming of this or that, talking about how he was close on a breakthrough project, but he would never talk about what the project was.

Momma tried to be encouraging as best she could, but even she knew after a while that Andy was never going to have a "breakthrough project." She just hoped he would keep one job and start a pension or get some extra money so they could get another car that would not break down each time she circled the block. Their family was growing, and she was worried that the car they had would not survive much longer. Andy. Andy left my momma there, with nothing more than a grocery store bag she had with her when her water broke, and a biting fear of what she would do next. I can see why Grandad and Grammy did not like Andy, and why they never liked to talk about "the dreamer."

Davey obviously never knew his daddy, just like me, but he at least knew his name. Maybe one day he could look him up and find him. I am not sure he would ever want to, and he really never talked about it. He just acted outright tough like it never mattered to him. That he was just fine on his own and would not even need a daddy to teach him lessons in life. I always had wanted one, but not if he was like Davey's dad. How a daddy could just up and leave like that, I never understood. My Momma was a good catch. She was pretty, smart, and she had goals of her very own too. Real goals, not these Andy made up goals. I mean, she even went to college. That was a goal and she had stuck that out. So, in my book, she was a million times better at goals than that Andy guy would ever be. Clearly, he had no idea who my momma was.

Andy happened to also be the daddy of Janet, but not Thelma Louise. Janet did not mind talking about him. She was two and a half when he left, so she did not remember him at all, but it just did not seem to bother her much. She loved Momma, and those two got along just fine without him. She never cursed him like Grammy did whenever his name came up, but she never talked good about him either. She just said things like, "I guess he had bigger plans," or "maybe he got lost in the parking lot and is still circling around trying to find the entrance again." She laughed when she said that, and I did too because it made her laugh.

I liked Janet. She never really got angry much, even without a daddy in her life.

Nope. She always found the good in everything. I wanted to grow up and be more like Janet, well, a boy version of Janet. Who was happy, smart, and did not care about not having a daddy. Oh, and I would not be wearing a suit. Just like Janet would not. That would be for certain.

Once I asked Grammy about my dad. I asked her if she knew his name, or what he had been like. She always tried to change the subject, and I never understood why. She would say, "Jasper, hey let's go in town and get some ice cream cones, just you and me. We can talk about that all later, what do you say?" Ice cream always sounded good, and besides, there was plenty of time to talk about it later, so I always went with the ice cream. Who wouldn't? My favorite was double fudge ripple, and Grammy always went with strawberry maple pecan.

Davey would go with us sometimes, but mostly it was me and Grammy. She liked to get out with just the two of us. It was Grammy and Jasper time, and she would treat me to two huge scoops if I had done all my chores that week, and sometimes even if I did not. I think she may have been bribing me, so she did not need to talk to me about my daddy, but I caught on. So, if I ever wanted double fudge ripple ice cream, I would ask Grammy about my dad. It became so I did not even care to know, but I knew it would most likely get me more ice cream. I tried not to do it too much. Grammy was smart, and I did not want her to catch on and spoil it for me.

Momma never talked about my dad either. She did not even talk about Andy. I overheard, one night while listening to Grammy and Grandad talk on the front porch, that old Andy had removed just about anything of value from the place they shared, dropped Thelma Louise and Janet off at the front walkway to Grammy and Grandad's house, drove some old pickup down to town, over the bridge, and out of sight. He never looked back even once, not even to say goodbye to the girls. He just drove and drove, and no one ever heard from him again. Grammy said he had family all over, and probably shacked up with one of his moron cousins who happened to not be in prison at the time. She had no idea I don't think, but she was just mad as a badger. What he did to her daughter put a sharp thorn in her side, and she left it there as a reminder to trust no one with her daughter again. That had ruined it for her.

Thelma Louise was the daughter of Louis "Lefty" Sheridan. Louis was an office type worker. He wore thin wired rim glasses, had a clean-cut face, and wore fancy suits daily at work. He was not very tall. Not very broad at all either, but Momma liked him anyhow. They met while in their senior year of high school, and Louis asked Momma to marry him rather quickly after they graduated. Momma was young, unsure, and she just felt it was what was the next stage in life, so she said yes.

When Thelma Louise was born, Momma surprised Louis by making her middle name a variation of his. He was a quiet man, but he smiled whenever he was really pleased with something. He smiled with this news from Momma. First, he was now a daddy for the very first time, and to have his daughter named after him, was something special. Real Special.

Lefty, named that because, well, he was left-handed, was a proud papa. He told all the workers at his office about how his young wife had named the baby after him, and so they all started teasing him and asking how his daughter "Lefty" was doing. He turned red with embarrassment but took it in stride. He was a very even-tempered man, and Momma loved that about him. They talked about buying their first home, raising more kids, and buying a pontoon boat for the river just south of town.

There was a spot near the banks of the river next to an old blast furnace that Momma and Lefty liked to go for picnics on weekends. It sat next to an old gray stone wall, covered now by thick green ivy growth, and had a thin water trickle running over. Momma would lay a blanket down and unpack the sandwiches and grapes and drinks she had packed, and they would sit with their shoes off talking about the future. Momma was a planner, so she loved nothing more than talking about the future and what they wanted to achieve. What they would do, where they would go, what color the curtains would be in the family room. All of it. Momma loved it all.

Momma and Lefty were unquestionably happy. Life was good for them. But that sadly and abruptly changed.

Louis Lefty Sheridan died suddenly while coming home from the office he had been working at, when Thelma Louise was just a mere 2 months old. His car was hit by a large gravel dump truck, causing it to careen off the asphalt road, down a steep embankment, and into the flowing river below. The same river they had planned to buy a pontoon boat for. The very same one they picnicked next to just a mile up the bank. Louis was just 20 years old, and when Momma got the news, she stared straight ahead, and passed out, dropping harshly to the floor. She was just so in shock from it all and could not believe the ghastly news. Her young husband, her daughter's daddy, and all her immense dreams she had shared with him, were all gone in one quick moment. That is all it took to change the course of her entire life. One moment. Everything would change for Momma after that, and she was determined to get things back on track for her and Thelma Louise.

Chapter 5

The Loss

* * *

The day Grandad passed, Grammy was keeping herself as busy as she could, talking to Momma about how she had to stain the front porch soon, wanting to fix the fence at the right rear corner of the yard that had sagged, and just about everything and anything else she could think of. Momma knew she was hurting deep inside and trying to cover that, so she just nodded and would say things like, "Mom, I think that is a good idea, we should get the wood for that fence and get to that later next week," Grammy would just nod in agreement and look around earnestly for more trivial projects, almost like in a trance. She continued to talk and fuss, and then Momma interjected,

"Mom, shall I make the calls to Serenity funeral home, to get Dad picked up and taken over? I can handle the calls and prepare the funeral, mom. I can do that."

"Yes, yes, that is fine. You do that. I want to get over to the lumber yard before they close and get that wood and that porch stain. People always pick off the good straight wood quickly. There is always so much to do around here, and I want to get a start on things. So, you handle that all, and I will get going on this."

Grammy walked over to her old dusty pickup truck, the one Grandad drove almost daily with her into town, opened the squeaking driver side door, looked off to the yard where Grandad had spent so many hot summers, and paused. She just stood there for a moment, seemingly collecting herself, and then she got in, started it up, and drove away. She wanted to just forget today. Forget the last few weeks, to be honest.

Grandad had been sick for several weeks, but he kept telling Grammy he would be just fine, and to not worry herself at all. He was a tough SOB, he told her. I had no idea what a tough SOB was, but he was whatever that was for sure. Smiling each day she was with him, he seemed perfectly content with it all. Only he knew the pain he was in, and he masked it well. Grandad knew Grammy, and Momma for that matter, needed to think he was okay. That he was going to by some means pull through, and that he was in no pain whatsoever. So, he continued to hide the savage pain he felt, and when the doctors told them it was getting close, that they should prepare for the inevitable worst-case scenario, Grammy was dumbfounded.

How was this possible? He was simply fine. He had told her that he was fine. There was no nagging pain, no type of discomfort through his sturdy body. In her mind, they were back home on the porch swinging lazily, talking about retirement one day. Speaking about how many grandkids they had hoped to have in their golden years. Sipping ice-cold lemonade, while bouncing the newest grandkid off their knees. But the truth was, Grandad knew. He knew his life was coming to a sudden end. He knew the pain was unbearable, and that at any moment, one of these hello's and goodbyes we all too often take for granted, would be the last to travel from his lips.

So, he decided when he knew what was to come, that he would make no one else suffer alongside him. He wanted to make those around him as happy and purely relaxed as he could, because he knew it would be hard. That was a terrible understatement. He was Grammy's reason for waking in the morning, and her reason she slept so peaceful at night, and she needed him. Momma needed him too, because she was raising us by herself, and Grandad became somewhat of a father to us all.

Grandad was a genuine, kind and strong man, and even though he carried around that horrible regret from all those years ago, he had been forgiving. Though he could never fully forgive himself. The parents of that little boy Frederick had known their son was hanging with a mischievous group of kids. They tried to keep him in that evening, but he snuck out once again through his narrow bedroom window. They knew, and they knew Grandad's family. The stories about him in the war doing unspeakable things to save those around him with such bravery, and how he was a good sturdy, honest family man.

They held no grudge, and although they missed their

boy, they fought for no charges to be pressed, and were somehow successful. Grandad was always amazed by this. He never understood how someone who had just lost a child, could feel so strangely forgiving to the man who had removed him from their world. But that was how it was. Now, he did not have to carry that guilt and sadness any longer. He did not have to feel sorrowful, or angry, or pain at all. He was free of all of that, but now we were all left sad, angry, and in pain. We missed him terribly.

Momma called Mr. Murphy at the funeral home, and I could hear her whisper to him a faint "thank you." My guess was that he was telling her he was sorry for her family's loss, as so many others would over the next week. People apparently say that when someone dies. Sorry for your loss. It seems honestly appropriate, but this was not just any rudimentary loss. This was Grandad. People needed him, and I do not think they understood that well enough. But Momma was nice anyway, even though she needed Grandad as much as Grammy did. I needed him. He gave me those pale silver cufflinks after all, and I still did not have the slightest idea how or when to wear them. He took me on long hikes through dry leaves and wet skies in the early fall when Davey and his pals would not let me tag along on those crisp spring days. Who would take me on those hikes now? Not Davey, that's for sure.

This was not good, and I was sad. Bitter. Momma needed me, though, so I tried to do some things while she talked on the phone. I dusted the dining room table to a shine, even though it did not look as if it needed any dusting. I went to the kitchen to fetch a hard-bristled broom so I could sweep the bare wood floor, where she could see me in plain view. I wanted her to see I was trying, that I could be the man of the house sure-enough, well, when Davey was not home. I could do it.

Maybe I could get a job and help pay the bills. Grandad told me how he had worked from the time he was just a little boy. Why couldn't I? A paper route, maybe. Just until I became a professional baseball player. Like Eric Davis. Just like him. Then I would make a ton of money and have my picture on one of those thin cardboard trading cards as Grandad called them. Kids would run to the store and hope to get my card with my picture on it. They wouldn't trade my card ever, though. Nope, they would keep mine in a small brown shoebox with the top tattered. I could buy Momma a house of her very own, and she could decorate it with gold colored flower print photos, and we could all live together forever in that house. Grammy could come along, and she would always tell people about her grandson Jasper, the professional baseball player for the Cincinnati Reds.

"Ronnie, do me a favor, please? Can you go in the other room and fetch Momma my pen and paper, please, honey?" Momma asked.

"Yes, Momma. I will and I'll be right back," I responded.

The church was Saint Augustine's. We had gone there each Sunday for as long as I could remember. It was a small humble church, featuring dull granite with slivers of silver and copper throughout from top to bottom, with a simple white crucifix at the peak. The doors were painted a deep red, and when you walked in, it always smelled funny. Like a cinnamon incense type of scent. Or maybe the holy water had a smell to it.

Either way, I knew the smell from the parking lot before we entered through the doors. When we walked in, everyone was quiet. There were a few older men standing around in the back, smiling, shaking hands, all wearing dark-colored suits. To the left of the center aisle were a few rows with people milling around in them, and then a seemingly on purpose break between people for several rows, then more people.

I walked to the very front with Davey, Janet, Thelma Louise, and Momma, who was leading the way. Momma looked at me, and straightened my tie, licked her fingers and placed them on top of my head with a slight push to pat my hair down, and told me to slide into my seat there in the hard wooden pews. I hated the tie. I hated the suit. Momma had a friend who leant it to her for me, because I did not own one of my own. It did not fit quite right, though. The collar crept upwards, and it was a little long in the sleeves, so I fidgeted with it all the way until we got to our pew. Then Momma told me to sit still, so I tried my best.

Davey played with his tie, cause he did not like them either. He kept loosening it with two fingers while stretching his neck as far from it as possible and Momma just kept tightening it. Janet and Thelma Louise wore printed dresses with flowers down the front and sides. Janet's was a pale-yellow dress with light pink flowers, while Thelma

Louise wore a white dress that had blue and green flowers on the bottom half, and a fancy gold stripe pattern around the top. They did not have to wear a stupid tie, and I felt that was unfair, but Momma told me girls did not need to wear ties. That was the only time I had wished I were a girl, so I did not need to wear a dumb stupid tie.

I looked over at the different people on the other side of the old church, and they were just looking straight forward, all quiet. I did not know what they were looking at until I looked up to the front of the church where the priest was calmly standing around. He wasn't wearing a tie either, though. Seems like many people weren't. Where he was standing, there was a long curved shiny wood box type of thing, and I was trying to see what was in it. I could not see from where I was seated, and the fact I was still small, so I asked Davey.

"Davey, what's in the box up there where that priest is?"

"Shhhhh," Davey said. "It's Grandad. Now sit and be quiet. I don't want Momma getting all upset again."

What did he mean that was Grandad? I thought he was dead. Maybe he was just playing with me, pulling my leg. I stretched outwardly towards the box to get a better look without standing, but the box was on top of some metal silver thing with small black wheels, and it was just too high for me to see. When Janet saw what I was doing, she switched spots with Davey, and slid down to where I was, leaning in towards me.

"Ronnie, it's okay. It's Grandad. When we die, they put us in a box like that one, called a casket. People can walk up and say their goodbyes this way, and then they close the lid and bury you in the ground. The box protects your body and lets you look handsome for those around you," she explained.

"Why, why does his body need to be protected? Isn't he already dead?" I asked, confused.

"Well, yes, he is dead, however, I don't know, Ronnie. I guess they just protect it, so when you go to visit them at the cemetery, you picture that they are still the same person they were when they died. Like they did not change. If they were all covered in dirt, they may be eaten by worms, and such. No one wants to picture them like that, right?"

She was right, but I had seen worms in my yard, and built them great big houses like those big palaces in town. I never had a worm try to eat me. I never even had a worm try to bite me. I don't think they have teeth. Do they? I was only getting more confused as the morning went on. Grandad was in that box, so people could say goodbye to him, although he could not say goodbye back. Then they would close the lid, and it would be all dark in there. Why did he need a suit on then? After that, they put the wooden box, or casket thing Janet had told me about, into the ground, covered it with dirt, and then left. Then people would still come by and say hi to him occasionally? None of it made any sense. Janet just held my hand tightly and told me to not worry. I would understand more when I got older. Momma was always telling me that. That I would understand more as I got older. Well, I wish I had a pad of paper to write all that stuff down, because someone would have a lot of answers to give me when I was old enough.

Grammy was talking to some old guys just a few rows away, and she was nodding a lot. She wasn't really talking as much as she was listening. Grammy always talked a lot. She always had things to say, but lately, she was not saying a whole heck of a lot. Here she was just nodding and listening. Her dress was deep black, below her knees, and she had a dark purple jacket over top. Her hair was naturally curly and shorter, but it looked like she had a fancier hairdo that day. It was still sterling gray, but it looked different.

She looked over our way and caught me staring at her. When she looked directly at me, she just winked nonchalantly, and turned back to the nodding and listening again. The men were holding hats in their fist, clenched tightly around the brims, and they were looking down at Grammy, because she was much shorter than they were. I remember they were all old looking, unkempt gray hairs going in different directions as if trying to avoid one another, and they wore dull shirts and dark print ties, but mostly no suits. One had an ashy colored green uniform on, and silver and gold looking pins on his chest. His hat differed from any I had seen before, but he still held it in his hands like the other men nearby. He was standing taller than the others, even though he was not the tallest, looking almost straight, but his eyes were lowered as Grammy just nodded.

When she finished talking to the men, she smiled at them, thanked them, and walked towards the row we were sitting in. Momma just looked at her when Grammy sat next to her and laid her head on Grammy's shoulder. Grammy put her hardened hands on her head and kissed it. They sat like that for a few moments, until the music started up. Then the priest started singing in a deep-toned way, but I could not understand what he was singing. He had a strange raspy voice, and it did not seem like words coming from his mouth, but I guess they had to be. He put his hand over Grandad's box, and looked down at him, and prayed.

Everyone else in the church bowed their heads. I did not, though. I just watched as I wanted to see what people were doing. Some people were sniffling as if they were about to shed tears, and some looked more like they were asleep. No expression whatsoever. I looked at Grammy and Momma. They were sniffling for sure. Even Thelma Louise was crying. Momma still with her head resting heavily on Grammy's shoulder, placed a free hand on Thelma Louise's hand, without looking in her direction, and held it tightly. Thelma Louise squeezed Momma tightly back and wiped away the tears from her eyes with her other hand. Davey was not crying. He had his eyes closed, and was looking down, but he was not crying. He looked like he was mumbling something to himself, but I could not really tell. Almost like he was talking to someone but didn't want anyone else around him to know.

Janet still had a soft grasp on my hand, and she had her head lowered, but she knew I was looking around. Maybe she felt my hand slightly move as I looked left and right and behind and to the front. She could feel I was fidgeting in place, so she just squeezed a little firmer. It was then I closed my eyes and said a prayer just like everyone else seemed to be doing. I wanted Grandad back, but I did not think that was the prayer to say. I just said, "God, take care of my grandad, and keep him safe. Please do not let the worms get to him, even though I do not know why they would want to. And keep Grammy happy. I know she misses him, terribly she does, so keep her safe. Momma and I need her."

When the priest was finished with his prayer and singing and talking, he asked if anyone wanted to come up and say a few final words about Walt. Funny, I had forgotten that was Grandad's other name. A man in a slightly wrinkled beige shirt, with a chocolate brown tie too short for his body, stood up, walked over to where the priest was, and asked the priest if it was okay to say a few words. The priest told him it was. He had literally just said that was what this time was for, so I was not sure why the man asked, but he did.

"Um, hello everyone. My name is Clint, Clinton Johnson. Um, I met Walt under awful circumstances for sure. My boy Frederick you see. Well, anyhow, Walt was a good man. He always tried his darndest to do whatever he could for people, and he was sure that way with me. For years, after I lost my only boy," the man paused here, and I thought for a minute he might not go on, but then he did go on.

"Walt would come by and do work on my house, even without my asking. He would fix a fence post or nail a loose board back up again for me or paint a shutter. He never wanted anything from me, that I had not already given him. He just kept doing this, for years. When we finally moved away, Old Walt asked if he could buy the house from us, and so, we thought that was a splendid idea. We figured he had already done so much work to the house, that it made sense to just give him the house for whatever he could afford. My wife and I are firm believers in giving back, and Walt, we just loved. Anyhow, um, I just wanted to say that." Then he looked over at Grandad, walked to the box, placed his hand on what I assume was Grandad's hand, and said,

"Walt, old buddy. You are free. It cannot hurt you anymore. I wish it never had. Will you do me this one favor? Will you say hi to Frederick for us? Tell him we are sorry, and we love him, and we will see him when it is our time. Can you do that for me, Walt? Thank You. Thanks."

He shuffled off, with painfully sad eyes all red and watery, and sat back down next to a woman who I assume was his wife. She smiled warmly at her husband and touched his cheek with the inside of her palm and then kissed him on his forehead. Then he smiled, and looked over at Grammy, and she nodded back and mouthed what appeared to be "Thank you." Only, I had no idea what was going on. I guess this was one of those times I would need to ask when I was old enough. I really needed a pad and pen. It was going on my list of things to do when I got back home.

A few more people went up, and they talked and told stories about times they remembered Grandad helping them, or about times they had worked together, or that time when he did this or that when the weather was bad and the roads were closed. People just told stories, and I knew none of them. I may have seen them in town say hi to Grandad while we walked side by side, but I knew none of these people well.

Then the man with the dull green suit, with the shiny metal things on his chest, and the different black hat, walked up. He did not look at anyone on his way to the front, he just looked straight ahead like he had purpose. He shook hands firmly with the priest, and turned around in a single strong motion, and at first looked where Grandad was, then back to the people. He was a medium-sized man, but he looked strong and notably serious. He did not smile, nor did he look upset. He just looked straight, and with a deep sturdy voice, he began,

"I'm Master Sergeant Hollingsworth, of the United States Army. I served with Corporal McFarland while overseas, back in 1942 and 1943. Corporal McFarland, Walter, was a good soldier, but a better man. We saw a lot of unbalance together while we were there, and we decided to leave what we saw there, behind us. Walter once told me that until he died, he did not want to ever mention what we had been through, and I said the same. It was not easy for us, and we were just boys trying to make our country safe and get home to our lives again. To our Families we left behind. Not knowing we were returning so different, so transformed, so full of emotions. Walter, he never wanted credit for anything he'd done. He simply wanted to do his job, get home to his wife, and raise a family. It is all he talked about, day and night."

The man in the green suit paused again and looked over

at Grammy this time. He began again,

"Ma'am, Your Walter, your Walt, he saved a lot of men. He saved me. We were pinned down deep. Enemy fire was whizzing all around, and we were running low on ammo. Walter was just north of us and knew we were under fire. It was getting dark except for the crimson sky, and old Walter had to act fast. Without thought for his own survival, he took as much ammo as he could carry, ran through enemy fire, over several dead soldiers that had already given their lives for the fight, and into the hole we were pinned down in. Walter dropped the ammo, and as we loaded, he quickly rose up, and fired round after round into the fading red night, screaming at the top of his lungs. He was angry. Angry that they had us pinned down and kept firing. He thought that was unfair, and even though it was a war, he still felt it was not right. Walter couldn't stand an unfair fight. By the time he was almost out of ammo, we had all loaded back up, and resumed the fight. It was enough, enough to save all of us, and Walter did not need to do that. He was in an advanced position, went against orders to stay put and stand down, and took his life in his hands, to save some guys from Iowa. I never forgot that. I would not be here..." for the first time, the man, who had been like a rock since walking into the church, had trouble speaking and standing as straight as he had just a moment before.

He did not continue. He simply walked over to Grandad, said something I could not hear, took one of the medal things he had on his chest off, and placed it where Grandad was laying. He then went over to Grammy, and he knelt down beside her, and said, "Ma'am, thank you for sharing Walter with us. I will never forget him, nor you for your generosity. I want to give you this." He took something from his top pocket, looked at it, rolled in around in his palm and between his thick fingers, then handed it to Grammy. "Please, accept this as a token of my appreciation. I am truly sorry for your loss."

Chapter 6

Coming Home

* * *

Momma certainly had her fair share of downfalls in her life, but she always seemed to manage a friendly smile, and to find the will to push through. After Lefty passed, she took some time to collect herself, moved in with Grammy and Grandad for a while, and then just about a year later, met Andy. She was still young, at just 22 years old, and believed she'd fallen deeply in love. Andy wasted no time asking Momma to marry him, despite Grandad and Grammy's concerns. He told Momma there was no sense in waiting for everyone else to agree with their decision if they already knew how they felt. Besides, Momma had a young girl she was raising, and he said he would step up and help her raise her child. He never wanted to discuss Lefty, or Louis as he would call him. No, this was a new life, and worrying about the past and what had already happened, both good and bad, seemed a huge waste to Andy.

Grandad and Grammy tried to talk to Momma, telling

her to take her time. That she was still very young, a pretty woman, and a mother to a little girl. She should be in no rush at all. If Andy truly loved her, as he said he did, they would have plenty of time to get married and have the family Momma always desired. Love would make sure of that. But Momma just did not listen well at all. She was in love, scared for her future and being alone, still mourning the loss of Lefty, and well, she wanted a larger family. She wanted to have more children and own a nice house with a good yard and different colored flowers on the front porch with a porch swing, and birthday parties with friends and all of that. She wanted a decent life, and this, in her mind anyway, was how to get that.

So, Andy and Momma went down to the courthouse, never telling Grandad and Grammy of their intentions, and got married in front of the front desk clerk at the court. Some old senile judge married them, with Momma in a soft, teal-colored dress with teal shoes, and Andy in his nicest pair of blue jeans and a button-down powder blue shirt. It was the only nice shirt he had owned. The ceremony, if that is what you could call it, lasted an entire 8 minutes, and Momma was legally married for the second time.

Momma found a place just in town, and Andy stopped by one afternoon, put a small deposit down, and they had a place to call their own. The rent was cheap, and it quickly became apparent why. The place smelled of mildew all the time, and the walls seemed to be paper-thin. They could hear all the other obnoxious tenants in the building talking and flushing their toilets. Momma hated it and felt horrible that she had been the one to find it, but she just wanted a place to call theirs. A place of their own.

Andy did not particularly care. He was always working on his ideas, his projects. When he did come home, Momma would find him sitting up on the dining room table, with papers spread out all over, jotting notes here and there and making drawings of something he just had to get out of his head. It wasn't that he didn't have good ideas. Not at all. It was that he had no idea how to get those ideas from his head, to paper, to fruition. He could not focus on just one thing at a time. One idea would start, and he would begin to draw a diagram with all sorts of numbers and lines around it, and then before he would move on to the planning phase, he would have another great idea, this one even better than the last and be drawing that one next. The last idea discarded and forgotten.

Their dining room table was always covered by half scribbled drawings, and lead penciled writings, and card-board cutouts. There was never room to actually eat at the table. Momma did not mind, though. She really had felt initially Andy would come through. He was smart, smarter than her, she thought. But Andy just did not have ambition. He had no drive. He would not take advice from people. He knew better than everyone around him, he felt. Eventually, Momma realized he was not going to ever get something from paper to reality, and the realization hurt her deep in her core.

Grandad would stop over weekly to check on things, or to offer a hand by watching the kids, so Momma and Andy could go out and spend some time together. He knew how important spending adult time alone was, and he rarely ever told Momma no. Grammy refused to come to the house until Andy agreed to remove the papers from the table. She just thought it was rude, and the fact he made them eat on the floor in the living room rubbed her the wrong way. Momma tried to explain to Grammy he was getting closer to a breakthrough and needed all the free space he could find, and Grammy would reply, "For cartoon drawings, he needs all the free space he can find?"

"Mom, they aren't cartoon drawings. You do not understand. He has all these amazing ideas, and yes, maybe he is a little scatter brained, but once I help him organize this all, one of these ideas is bound to take off and he will provide a much better home for us and the kids. That I know. He told me he is getting closer every day. I believe him, Mom. I have to."

Grammy wanted Momma happy, so she would invite them over for supper. She was, however, sticking to her guns. She would not be eating on the floor of that old run-down apartment. It was simply out of the question. They would just eat at Grammy's place. That was that.

Grandad tried to talk to Grammy about it, but it was no use. He understood her reasoning, but he would still stop by whenever he could. His grandkids were there, and his daughter, and if she needed him, well, he would be there for her. Grandad knew Momma just wanted a fair shake at life. She wanted to find her own way to a normal, happy life and she would work for it.

When Andy was not bringing home a steady paycheck, Momma would find extra work. When Andy thought he had a sure thing idea and needed some capital so he could get things rolling, Momma would find extra work. She backed Andy with all she had and tried hard to keep Grammy and Grandad and Andy all happy at the same time. She just wanted to be happy, Momma. Andy, though, always seemed to want more than he was giving. Momma was getting frustrated after some time, and Andy could not understand this.

One day he would make them filthy rich, and she was giving him grief? It made little sense to him, but not a lot made sense to Andy. He felt you were either with him or wanted to see him fail. There was no in-between in his eyes. Momma sincerely wanted him to succeed in the worst way, and she had faith in him, but she also had sense about her. She knew that things were tight, and that if he continued to take all her hard-earned money for his ideas, and they continued to go nowhere, they would be even worse off. She was not willing to sit idly and let that happen. After all she was the one working to pay the bills, put food on the table, and pay the babysitter each time she went to work. It was like she could never get ahead, no matter how many hours she worked.

So, when Andy decided not to stick it out, and took what little they did have, including that dining room table, Momma was hurt but not surprised. She had given it all she had, and despite her best efforts, she simply could not make things work alone. At least she could stop giving him money for his half ideas that she knew in her heart, were going nowhere. She was embarrassed when she had to tell Grammy, but Grammy never made a fuss. In fact, Grammy never said much at all.

She knew her daughter was a hard worker, with a big heart and someone with the best intentions, even if she was thick-headed and did not take the advice Grammy knew was right. She knew Momma had to learn things for herself, to grow. It was these lessons, she thought, that would help Momma make better-informed decisions in the future. These lessons that would allow Momma to maybe listen to Grammy and Grandad a little more when they told her what they thought. Grammy knew she had not always made the best decisions, so she knew Momma would not always make them either. Momma knew Grammy did not like Andy. She knew she was so angry at him that if she saw him after this, she would staple his tongue to the roof of his mouth, but she also knew that Grammy loved her. That Grammy was proud of Momma for all she had already been through at such an early age.

When Momma lost Louis, she was confused, and lost on how to make the next steps in her life. She hurt, and just wanted a better life. Louis, although so young when they married, was a decent hardworking man with plans. He did not just have ideas. No sir, he implemented them. He knew at a very young age, just how to take an idea, write it down, get it going and make it a reality. Momma had loved that about Louis, so when he was gone, she saw that in Andy and just latched on. There was no way for her to know Andy was not Louis. That he had not the drive nor the abilities of Louis. Maybe that is why Andy never wanted to hear about him. Maybe he was jealous, that Momma had someone who knew how to do what he did not. Maybe he knew Momma still loved Louis and missed him, although she tried not to bring him up in front of Andy. Maybe, he just knew, he would never measure up.

Momma, after delivering Davey, went over to the apartment with Grandad and his truck. When they opened the dingy front door, there was nothing but some scattered papers on the floor, a broken desk lamp with no shade in the corner, and an old orange and brown chair, ripped and beaten, where the TV had once been. Her clothes were still in the closet, but the kid's clothes were all gone. The plastic hangers remained firmly in the closets, but nothing else. In the kitchen, she saw that the cups were gone, the dishes, and even the food. Only one frozen dinner was left, but there was no microwave to cook it in regardless. Momma was hurt, painfully embarrassed, and so confused by it all. How could a man who claimed he loved her and her children, who she had worked extra jobs, extra hours, to help support his dreams that had no way of going anywhere, leave a place they once shared, in such a horrible state? Why would any man do this, she thought to herself?

She walked in, and looked around, wanting to retrieve something, anything, that would make her feel this trip to the apartment was not a total waste of Grandad's time. Grandad just put his arm around her and pulled her close. He whispered to her,

"Honey, it looks worse than it is. Look, he left some of his drawings. Maybe the ones he left were the better of his harebrained ideas, you never know."

Momma laughed, even though she did not want to. Grandad was right, though. Maybe this wasn't the worst thing that could have happen. Her first husband had died, and things were just sudden. This? This marriage had been dying since it started. Before even. Andy was obviously selfish, and she would not need to work for his ideas anymore. She could now simply work for her and her three kids. She would find a way to work it all out and make her life matter. She still had all her dreams and goals, and Andy leaving would not change any of that. No, she would not let him take that from her. That was something, he simply could not touch. She would succeed, and he would see her one day and know he had messed up badly and discarded a good woman. Momma made that a promise to herself. That she would do great things and he would see that.

When the landlord walked in, he noticed Momma sad and Grandad consoling her.

"Ma'am, sir, is everything alright? Is there anything I can do? Do you need me to call the police?" he asked sheepishly.

Grandad looked over his way, and just shook his head no. He never said a word, and the landlord just backed out, without turning around, and pulled the door closed.

"Dad, if we can just grab my clothes and go, that would be good," Momma said.

Grandad told her to go sit in the truck, and that he would handle it. She need not worry, he would get everything she needed, and she would not need to see that dirty old place filled with terrible memories ever again. He was always trying to fix things, and Grandad was good at that. He was certainly not going to allow his daughter to sit there, looking at what some dumb, stupid, selfish man had left her with, and cry.

Momma took her head off Grandad's shoulder, went to the doorway, and for just a second thought about turning around for one last look, but then thought different of it. She put her head up to the top of the door, looked out of the apartment, took one immense deep breath, and walked down to Grandad's truck. She opened the door, and sat there, waiting for Grandad to finish. He made two trips. That was all he needed. Two trips to collect all she owned now. All she and her three young kids had to their names.

Once he gently placed the belongings in the back of the truck, he covered them with an old wool blanket, went back up to lock the door, which probably did not need to even be locked at this point, and went over to where the landlord was pretending to be doing busy work.

"Umm, hey. So, she's not going to be needing that apartment anymore." Grandad began. "What is the remaining time left on her lease? What do they still owe to get out of that?"

The landlord looked as if he were thinking of when they had signed the lease, and calculating the numbers in his head, then he said to Grandad,

"If you can pay through the end of next month, I think that would square things away. I can get another tenant in.

Just that, and a fee for a cleaner to come in, and we will call it even," he replied to Grandad.

Grandad reached deep down into his back pocket, took out a weathered black wallet that had seen better days for sure, opened it, and gave the man enough to cover the current month, the next month, and extra money to cover a cleaner, although it wasn't like the place was clean when Momma had first moved in. Grandad was just elated to get Momma out of the lease and be done with it.

When he finished, he shook the man's hand firmly to seal the deal, put his tattered wallet back in his back pocket, and walked down to where Momma was sitting in the truck, looking straight ahead. He opened the driver door, looked straight ahead as well, and told Momma,

"I think it best you and the kids come and stay with me and your mom for a while. You know, just until you find another place of your own again. There will be no rush at all. We love the kids, and well, Grammy would love nothing more than to have them over there with her. She could watch them while you work. It would save you money on a sitter, and we could cook supper, so you did not need to rush home and do all of that. What do you think DeeBee?"

Neither was looking at the other. They both just kept staring straight ahead as if they were fixated on the same marvelous creation in front of them, and finally, Momma broke her stony silence.

"Dad, I'm sorry. I'm sorry I did not listen to you and mom. I'm sorry I rushed into things with Andy, and now you and Mom need to bail me out yet again. I promise,

Dad, I will do better. I will pay the rest of the rent, and as soon as that is all done, I will find another place and make it work. For now, yes, I think the kids would love to stay with you guys. It would help me a lot, Dad. A lot."

"Well," Grandad continued, "I spoke with the landlord and it turns out he did not want any more money. He just said he would get a renter right away, so there was no final payment needed. He is letting you out of the lease. So, let's just go home and we can figure this all out later. We have lots to do, and the attic rooms to set up for the girls. We can worry about this another time."

Momma, I think, knew Grandad had handled the final payment on her apartment, but he would not take credit for that, at the expense of Momma's sturdy pride. He was not the type of man to take credit. No, he was more worried about his daughter and those grandbabies of his. What he had done was simple, and a small, rather insignificant gesture as he saw it. Though it was significant to Momma for sure, it was more important for him to let her have her peace and her dignity. He wanted Momma to have one less thing on her mind. Grandad knew Momma would worry and find a way to pay him back, even if he protested repeatedly, so he figured if he did not tell her, he was killing two birds with one stone. That was Grandad. He had excellent timing and incredible insight into what was best. Once again, he made Momma feel like she mattered and was not a liability. She was his daughter, and he would ensure she had the help she needed, even if she would not ask for it.

Chapter 7

Ice Cream

* * *

When we got back to Grammy's house after Grandad's funeral, Grammy gently sat down on the front porch, looked out over the slightly overgrown yard, and took off her shoes. Momma told us to just let her be for a while. She said Grammy needed some time to herself to reflect, and even though I did not know what reflect meant, I knew Grammy needed to just be alone. I wanted to go out and hug her. Sit on her lap and tell her how much I missed Grandad, but Momma asked me to help her in the kitchen. Momma was crying most of the ride home, and her eyes were swollen, outlined in a fierce fire red, and covered in a sheen of clear liquid gloss.

"Momma, when do they put the dirt on Grandad's box? Do they do that at night, so no one sees? When do they, and when do we get to visit with him again?"

I had no idea of any of that. What death actually meant, was a mystery to me entirely. Maybe we would visit him, and he would be awake, but could not come home with us.

I didn't know exactly how any of that worked. Momma would know better, and so I asked her.

"Ronnie, Grandad is dead. So, we will not be visiting him anytime in the way you may think, honey. When things settle down some, I will drive you over to where he is, and we will talk about it more. Momma's a little tired right now, and I just want to get some food out on the table. Grammy needs to rest and take some time to figure out what she does from here. Okay, Ronnie?"

Well, it would need to be okay because again, I just knew I would not get any answers. So, I went to my bedroom and sat down at the edge of the bed. I undid my tie and threw it across the room and onto the floor next to where my dresser was. I sat there and thought for a good while. Then, I decided to go and ask Janet if she would give me some paper and a pencil. Maybe I needed to start my list of things I would expect everyone to answer when I was older. Grandad had died and so I already lost the answers he owed me. I wanted to write them down, so I would remember each and every one. When people from now on told me "When you get older, Ronnie, you will understand better," I would be sure they were kept to that. When I got older, I would pull out my list and go to each of their houses and read them aloud. They would have no choice but to finally give me all the answers, all the secrets they now kept from me for some strange reason.

Janet looked around the room, and in one of the drawers of her dark wood homework desk, she pulled out a small, emerald green colored spiraled notebook. It was no more than 6 inches high, and 4 inches wide. It was perfect, though! I could put this in my back pocket, and pull it out anytime someone said, "Ronnie, when you are older, you will understand better." She gave me a blue ink pen to go with it and said, "Here, Ronnie. Will this be good? I think it's a great idea, you writing down your notes and questions and all. It will make things a bit easier for you to remember this way, Ronnie."

I ran back downstairs swiftly, missing the bottom three steps altogether, over to where my room was, shut the door, and opened the spiraled green book to the first page. On that first page, I wrote:

"Ronnie Jefferson McFarland Jr., Jasper to my grammy."

Then I figured all the things Grandad had told me to ask when I was older, should go first. The problem was I had forgotten them and could not recall even one. I wanted to ask Grandad, but he was dead, Momma said, and we would not be visiting him for a little while, so I had to wait to ask him. I still had no idea how that was going to work, but I knew that I would talk him into coming back home. He loved his home with Grammy, and him and I needed to do our hikes, and our walks in town where everyone said "Hey Walt, lovely day today, isn't it? How is the Misses?" He would miss those conversations, so he would see my side of things and come back. Then he and I could sit down and write out those questions together. He would remember them more than I had. I just knew he would. He told me when I was older, I would understand, so he would surely remember at least most of them, I figured.

As I was finishing writing out my name, my eyes grew heavy as if they were fighting the notion of remaining open any longer. I grew so weary I dropped the pencil onto my bed, and it rolled out of my fingers and on to the floor. The spiral notebook slipped from my small palms and ended up on the floor as well. I laid back and fell into a deep sleep. The day had drained me, even though I had not felt it earlier. It had all just caught up to me at once, and I was missing Grandad more than I realized. Maybe when I got up from this deep trance, things would go back to how they had been just weeks prior. Maybe someone would answer my questions, even though I was still just a young boy. Maybe they would feel bad and know I was just being curious, as boys so often were.

"Jasper, Jasper are you okay?"

It was Grammy. She was sitting just on the edge of my bed where I had just sat down, running her fingers through my thick hair, looking down at me.

"Grammy? I must of fell asleep," I said as I rubbed both of my eyes. "Where is my notebook? My spiral notebook was right here, and I was going to put all the questions I had in there, so that when I grow up, everyone will tell me all the things they told me to wait for. It was right here."

"Jasper, it's right here, don't you worry. You will have all the time you need to fill that notebook up, and one day you will have the answers you were promised. I know Grandad was so proud of you, Jasper. He took a special liking to you. Him and you had a bond, and all the way until the moment he died, he made me promise to look after you.

He worried about you, and knew you had some trouble fitting in with your brother, but that will change with time. Jasper let's say you and I go for a ride in Grandad's truck. Would you be up for that?" Grammy asked.

I was up for it for sure. I put my black dress shoes back on, did not bother to change what I had on from the mass service we just had, but left my tie on the floor where it belonged. Then I grabbed my spiral green notebook, and before I got up, I asked Grammy,

"Is it alright if I bring my notebook? I might have a question that you cannot answer today, and I do not want to forget it. I want to be sure I write everything down Grammy. Will that be okay?"

Grammy looked at me, pushed her fingers gently and softly through my hair once more, and said nothing. All she did was wink at me, and I knew, that was a yes.

We walked out of my room, and past the kitchen where Momma had been a little earlier. I looked for her, but she was no longer there. Grammy did not wait for me to ask, she just said,

"Your Momma went to lie down. She had a rough time these past few weeks with Grandad. That was her daddy, and she had to be strong for me. Strong for Grammy. It is now time that I become strong, and let your momma have her time to grieve properly. Everyone needs their time to grieve Jasper. We all do it in very different ways, at all different times. Me? I usually grieve alone. So, don't you think I am ignoring you, or not paying much attention. I am. Always, I am. I just needed some time to think about things.

Grandad and I had so many wonderful years together, and a few we had to spend apart. It was not always easy, but he always took good care of me, and I took good care of him.

Our life together, it was a balance, Jasper. A balance is so important to a good strong healthy relationship. Some days you are strong, and some days you are drained, and weak. On the strong days, you give more. On the weak days, your partner gives a little more. Grandad was the type that had more strong days than weak days, but the weak days he did have, especially near the end, I gave more. I gave all I had to him, knowing his time was near. That is what we do for each other Jasper. Now, let's go get in Grandad's truck, and take it into town. We can grab some ice cream and walk around like we do when we want to be together alone. Do you know when you and he would go into town, he always came home, and told me he felt 10" tall when he walked next to you? Did you know that you made him feel so proud Jasper? Did you?"

We got in his truck, and Grammy touched the steering wheel with purpose, placing her hands tightly around it, but instead of starting the truck, just sat there. She sat there, just as he and she had done so many times, and she looked about, without saying a word. She looked at his dashboard and ran her old worn hands across it. She looked at his radio that he always had the news playing so soft you could barely hear it, and at the windshield, with a spider web crack Grandad refused to get fixed. He used to say that if you fixed everything that was broken, you would never live life. We would always find things to fix, looking at things that weren't really broken, but just not perfect, and want them perfect. The crack had grown over the months, and then over the years, but he just refused to fix it, even when people told him he should. That just made him not want to fix it even more. He would smile and say things like, "That there windshield is just fine as she is. I can see right through her, and isn't that what they are for? She's not bothering me, so I won't be bothering her."

Grammy eventually sat back, put the dull-looking bronze-colored key in the ignition, and started his truck. It took a little bit to turn over, but it eventually did. She moved the lever on the column down a few, and hit the gas pedal, and we were off. We drove down the road, and over the bridge. Down the main road, into town. The drive was short, but it felt like it took forever. People along the road looked over, recognizing Grandad's truck, and for a second, wondered if they would see him. When they remembered he was no longer alive and that it would be impossible to be him, they knew it had to be Grammy.

Everyone waved shyly her way, although I do not know that she saw any of them. She was just driving and thinking to herself, and in her own little world. She was grieving as she had said, in her way. I just looked out the passenger window, at all the places Grandad had pointed at over the years and dreamed about what it had looked like through his eyes. Where once there stood a proud bakery, now stood a strip mall with stores everyone saw in any other town. Where once he played stickball on a dirty field, now there were new homes waiting for new owners. Nothing was quite the same, and Grandad missed it the way it once was.

"Grammy, can I ask a question?"

"Oh, sure Jasper, I'm sorry. What is it?" she replied.

"Grammy, do you think Grandad is somewhere where he can have all the places he loved as a boy? Like, can he be playing stickball whenever he wants? Do you think he can walk around and start over, doing all his favorite things?"

"Jasper, that is a very good question."

I was hoping she was not going to tell me I would understand when I got older. In case she was, I had my green spiral notebook with me. My blue ink pen was in my hand now, and I waited. Thankfully, she answered as best she could.

"Well, Jasper. I do not know for certain, but I guess strangely, anything is possible. Grandad was a good, good man. If he asked God to go back to that time, a time when he was so happy in his life and the pace he lived was slower and more comfortable for him, I think it is possible that He could grant that to him. Do you understand death Jasper? Do you understand why we cannot see Grandad again?"

I had to think about that question. I put my head down into my chest, and closed my eyes for a moment, squeezing them tightly, so I could think real hard. I started to talk before I opened them, and replied,

"Well, Grammy, I don't know for sure. I know Grandad is going in the ground, and they are going to cover him with dirt. I know he stopped talking and was put in that big brown box, cause I saw that at the church. I saw them close the top, and he was still in there. Janet told me a little on the way back home, and she seemed to understand. I wanted to go visit Grandad and she said someday we could, but that even though he would be there, he wouldn't be there. That part is confusing, but I think we won't see him again, is that right, Grammy?"

We had come to the red light at the beginning of the stores in town. Grammy looked over at me, smiled and said,

"Jasper, that was really good. You are a lot smarter than your age, and that is a good thing. Janet was right in a sense."

"What sense was she right in, Grammy?"

"Well, she was right that we can go visit him soon, but that he will not be there. His body will be there. Always. He is buried there now, but his spirit, the part that made Grandad, Grandad, is no longer with him the same. So, he will not be there, the way we had known him to be."

"Well, where is his spirit now? Is it up in heaven? Is that where Grandad is? He is with God, isn't he, Grammy?" I asked, although I was pretty sure from what the priest at church had said, that I was right.

"Yes, Jasper, he is with God. He is looking down right now I'd bet, watching you and I go to the ice cream store, to get ice cream. He is smiling because this is exactly what he wanted for you. To do the same things that brought happiness to you and him. We are doing exactly what he would be doing today, so he is smiling down on us, Jasper."

I smiled gently, knowing he was watching me. It made me feel better knowing he was not totally gone, but just somewhere I could no longer see him. While that was sad for sure, at least he could watch me. I promised myself that

I would be good, so Grandad would be proud of me. That he could walk around heaven, feeling ten feet tall, because he was proud. I could do that for Grandad. For all he did for me, I could do that.

We got to the end of the street where the ice cream store was, the one Grammy and I had been to countless times and parked. When we got out of Grandad's truck, people looked over and nodded in our direction. It seemed they were saying hello, without saying it, and Grammy nodded politely back. When we got into the store, I ordered my double fudge ripple cone, and she ordered her strawberry maple pecan, on a cone as well. The man behind the counter prepared the cones, handed them to us with a broad smile, and when Grammy tried to pay, he said,

"These are for Walt today Ma'am. I'm sorry for your loss. Have a good day."

Everyone loved Grandad. Even the guy at the ice cream store behind the counter. Even he loved my grandad in a way that made me realize, he was much more than just a grandad.

Grammy smiled, and thanked the man, and told him that Walt was thankful for the gesture. The man smiled in a way that showed he did not want any attention for simply giving out ice cream cones, but that he was still grateful just the same. He felt it was the least he could do for Grandad, Grammy and me. We had been in there so often over the past year or so, and I am sure Grammy and Grandad had been in there about a million times over the span of their lives.

We walked back outside, sat on the only bench in front of the store, and ate our ice cream cones. We did not talk really, just sat there, looked around, and took licks of the double fudge ripple and strawberry maple pecan. Grammy pushed her cone my way, and offered me a lick, without saying a word. I took a bite and did the same in return. We just sat. For about ten minutes, we watched cars go by, people running to here or there, and babies crying in strollers. We watched men shaking hands across the street in suits, and women hugging each other as if they had not seen each other in a very long time. People were living their lives, although Grandad was not. It was all strange but it showed me something. People die, and other people still need to get on with their lives. Even if they did not want to. Grammy probably did not want to, but she did. She had to, and Grandad had made her promise to.

I wanted to ask Grammy so many questions, but I was just watching her gaze around at the street and watch people. I did not want to upset her any more than she already was today. The questions could wait until later. I could write my questions in my spiral book, and ask another time, when Grammy had done more of her grieving.

Chapter 8

Time for Class

* * *

When she and Grandad got home, Momma moved herself and the three kids she had at the time, into the furthest back room of Grandad and Grammy's house. There, she laid out some old blankets she found in the attic onto the hard floor, piled some clothes Grammy had given her for us kids neatly in piles on the floor under the window, and gasped as the sunlight kissed her cheeks. She was happy to have this place, her childhood home, as home again for now, but she was feeling as if she had let her kids down once again. She felt as if she had let her parents down, and that she had let herself down. How did this all happen? How was she the single mom of 3 young children, all under the age of 6, and living back with her parents, while she was still legally married to someone who had simply vanished into thin air? Had she been so naive to think that she could actually make her dreams work?

Maybe it was time to simply accept defeat, and just live

a simple life, pass that simple life onto her children, and live more for the moment, instead of reaching so hard for the future. She was feeling overly depressed and needed time. Time to find herself. Time to figure out just what was to come next in her path, and time to reflect on where she had already been.

Grandad walked into the room, having pulled a chair from the dining room table, placed it on the floor just inside the doorway, and sat down in the glow of that same sunlight Momma had allowed to warm her face. He did not look at Momma directly, because he knew she was hurting, and embarrassed. He just sat in the chair and stared down at the pile of blankets she had placed neatly and purposefully on the hardwood floor, to make a bed for her and her kids.

He was actually proud of Momma. Here was this young struggling woman, who had just delivered her 3rd child as her husband just up and left her all alone, with only the clothes on her back and some scraps of paper with silly diagrams and numbers scribbled on them. Here she sat, refusing to relent. Refusing to fold under the incredible pressure she felt. She was not throwing her hands in the air begging for relief as she grasped at the sky or sitting in a puddle sobbing over past mistakes. No, his daughter, his baby, was a strong willed, determined survivor and Grandad admired her perseverance.

"Honey, listen. Me and your mom have been talking, and well, we decided we are going to turn the attic into a room for you. Maybe the girls can stay there if you like, and you and David can stay down here. Your mom took the truck into town, and she's picking up a few things as well for you and the kids along the way. Now, we don't want any fussing over this. We know you desire to be independent and strong, but this is what we can do, so we will just do that. Look sweetheart, I know things are going to be tough for a little while, but everyone hits the bottom of the barrel at one time or another. I did, many years ago, back when I still had a drink or more in me. I could have lost all I worked so hard for, including your mom. But, for whatever reason, things did not go that way. I look back now and wonder why I was able to get through all that, and the answer was simple. All the people that supported me, guided me...forgave me. I'm not even sure I deserved that grace, but it was there regardless of what I felt I deserved. So, honey, please, take the support. Let us guide you as best we can. And forgive. Forgive yourself. For right now, forgive yourself."

Momma started to cry and got up from the blankets she had finished spreading out. She slowly walked over to Grandad, who was still looking down at his feet, and began,

"Dad. I am sorry. You and Mom are always there for us. You have always been, and I know that. I just want to make you proud and make my children proud. I know I have so much to offer, but I keep getting stuck in the mud, and I can't seem to move as quickly as my mind tells my legs to go. I just need to take my time, and I will be okay. I'm happy to take your hand here. I need it, truth be told.

As long as you know, it will only be for as long as we absolutely need it."

"Well, honey," Grandad said, now looking at his daughter's sad, but a little more relieved face. "You may be stuck in the mud some, but that just means you need step out of the heavy boots you've been wearing and find yourself a new pair of boots. Find new boots, honey. Find better boots."

Momma knew what he meant. She knew he was referring to her dreams and her ability to chase them. He was telling her to kick a little more, walk a little faster, push just a little harder and leave all the bad times and poor decisions behind. Never had he tried to discourage Momma from her dreams. No, he would never do that. All he had wanted was for her to be genuinely happy, and he would do just about damn near anything he could to ensure that she was. That was, at least how he thought, his purpose in her life. To guide her, push her in the right direction, and back her as best he knew how. When she needed him to let her go, he would follow closely behind and watch, without her knowing. When she needed someone to walk beside her because she was scared, he would be there to take her hand and guide her through, showing no fear. But when she needed him to take the lead, when she felt she had simply no more to give, that she was at her very end, he would take the lead and push whatever it was blocking her way clear out of her path with reckless intent. That, that was her dad. That was my grandad.

Time went on, and Grammy and Momma set up the tiny room, adding polka dot curtains to the windows, a small round paisley area rug to the floor, and a twin bed for Momma, plus a small wooden crib for little Davey. Grandad worked every night on the attic, and after a few weeks and some bumps and bruises, he had built a wonderful, perfectly adequate bedroom for the girls. Janet and Thelma Louise picked out sheets for their very own beds, the first they had of their own, and they were excited more than ever. Thelma Louise picked out a deep purple color, while Janet went with a hot pink, which matched her girlie personality. They both had a new wardrobe of slightly used clothing Momma had picked out at the secondhand store in town, but they did not know any better. To them, they were rich for the first time. New soft sheets that smelled just heavenly, new light oak wood post beds, AND all new clothes for each? They felt as if they had hit the jackpot, and in some sense, they had.

Andy was never going to amount to much, and Momma knew this. She needed to get out and start over fresh, and as sad as she was with how it all happened, it was what was she needed. She knew this, even if it did not feel right at that particular moment. Grammy and Grandad knew this as well. Over time, the kids knew this. They rarely asked about Andy, and as time went on, they just knew that they were being raised by the three people they loved more than anything in the world. Not everyone got that lucky, they thought to themselves. It was never about having a mom and dad for them, in the traditional sense of the word. It was about having the best people they could think of, and that they had without question.

Momma started to work more steady hours, and Grammy watched the kids while Grandad helped however he could. Grandad heard that a local community college was offering classes year-round, and he talked to Momma about enrolling there. He knew it would add to her already hectic life, but it could be just the break she so desperately needed. Maybe, if she could take a few classes here and there, she could get an associate degree, and then get a better paying, more permanent type of job, that would allow Momma to get on her own once again. He did not care that she stayed there, and he preferred it, but in his heart, he knew Momma wanted to get on her own two feet once again, to build a life separate from theirs, and he understood her immense desire for that completely.

When he mentioned the classes to her, Momma immediately questioned it. What about the money it took to attend? How about the hours she would need to devote to the class schedule? When would she see her children if she was working full time and attending classes? While it was something that she thought she could really do, there was an awful lot to figure out.

The following week, Momma took a ride over to the school and sat outside for a few moments wondering what she was doing there. She did not have the extra money for schooling, but apparently, they had grants from what a friend had told her, and all she needed to do was apply. So, she walked through the old, large dark wood carved doors leading into the community college of Aberdeen County, and went to the first desk she saw.

"You can apply for the grants we offer, and if you need more, we can help you secure loans as well. If this is something you really wish to do, we will work together and find you a way to make it happen," the man at the desk told her.

Momma never had any type of loan in her life, so she was unsure of how that all worked, but she was trusting, and determined. The people at the college were extraordinarily helpful, and they sat with her, helped her fill out the piles of forms for the loans and grants they offered and told her they would turn them in to the proper departments and contact her once they heard back. Momma thanked the man over and over, then she smiled, gathered her purse, and walked out of the school and down the road back to where she parked her car. As she drove back to her job, she daydreamed and wondered if this was the right move. Adding more to her already full plate, but it was exciting and she had submitted the applications, so it was done.

This could be the start of something wonderful, she thought to herself. Her dream of doing what she had always yearned for, being on her very own once again, and giving her children everything that she could afford to, was now in the works. She could feel that things were within her grasp, and all she needed to do was start. She knew how to start. It was the finishing she was not familiar with, but with all that time between starting and finishing, she knew she could figure it out.

If her mom and dad were serious about stepping in even more than they had done to this point, maybe she was right to take them up on their offer. Maybe she could pay them back, by getting things in order for her and for her children, and then they could get back to the dreams they had for themselves. Although, it seemed as if they were living vicariously through her for some reason. That having the grandkids around, was somehow bringing them back to another time, long ago, when they were much younger and more able to do the things they now only talked about.

Grandad was only three years away from retiring and collecting his pension. He was now in charge of the shipping side of the steel plant, which was a huge responsibility, but not the back-breaking work he had done for so many years. He was undoubtedly slowing down, and that work was just too hard on his worn and battered frame. Lately, he had talked more about fishing with "the boys," than he did about working. For many years he talked all about American steel. How the unions were protecting him and the other guys, and how vital they were to the future of the American family. Now, he barely mentioned the plant at all.

I think he knew, in his heart, that he was on his way out. They had offered to keep him on board in different areas of the plant, but Grandad had done all he wanted to for the company, and although he was grateful for the opportunity there, he was even more grateful for the fact he would get to spend the rest of his days casting a silk line with his grandkids, hooking a bass, and teaching them how to remove the hook from the mouth of the fish so it may live to fight another day.

To him, that was living. The kids would not want to hear about how steel had shaped America, and the shipping they did all over the globe, and how the price of steel was going up and companies were charging more for their products because they were paying more for the steel. No. Kids wanted to talk about sports, and who hit a walk-off homerun the night before to win the game. Or what size catfish they snagged down at the crick.

After a few short weeks of waiting, Momma found herself more impatient and felt that maybe the college had not accepted her application, or perhaps she did not get the grants or even the loans, and that the man behind the desk did not want to let her down. She started to seriously doubt her decisions, and just then, the phone rang. Grammy answered it and she said,

"Hello? Yes, she is here. Who should I say is calling? Well, oh, okay. Just one moment please."

She looked back and saw Momma standing behind her. She put her hand over the receiver, smiled and said,

"Honey, it's some young man from Aberdeen Community College. He wants to talk with you."

Momma walked over, took the phone from Grammy, and she too held her hand over the receiver. She closed her eyes, inhaled deeply, and then removed her hand and put the phone next to her ear.

"Hello? Yes, this is she. Oh. I see. Okay, yes, no thank you. I understand. Thank you for calling."

She hung the phone up, and looked down at first, as if she was trying to comprehend what had just happened on the phone, then looked up and over at Grammy.

"Mom," she began. "I was accepted. They gave me a

grant for the first year, entirely. I do not need any loans. As long as I keep a 3.5 grade point average, I can reapply for another grant. Mom, this is it. I start in three weeks!"

She looked stunned, but happy, nonetheless. Grammy went over to her and put her arms around Momma's neck. She pulled her close, kissed her on the top of her head, and just hugged her. Momma cried, but for the first time in a long time, her tears were tears of happiness, instead of warm tears of pain. All her hard work, her suffering, her inability to get ahead, would finally be in the rearview mirror as she looked back only to see where she had come from. She would finally have the opportunity to do something about her life, and she would control the outcome. That was perfect for Momma, because she was such a hard-working woman, and having no one in her way but herself, was exactly how she wanted it. She knew she could do this, and if she did not, it would be because of her, and not some man who promised the world and delivered nothing close to that.

When Grandad came home, Momma ran over to him to tell him the news. He was grinning from ear to ear. This was the best news he had heard in a while, and he too was excited that Momma now controlled her destiny. When he learned that she did not even need a loan for the first year, he sat down in his chair, looked up, and thanked God softly. He was so happy for her, and this grant meant she did not need to worry as much. She could focus more on her schooling and cut some hours from her work. That is exactly what she needed. Her boss was good, but she was exhausted, and this would have only added to that. Now though, it was a non-factor. She was starting school, and no one could stop her. Today was a great day.

Chapter 9

The Picnic

* * *

Grammy picked back up where she left off. She got right to repairing the tattered fence. She stained the weathered deck again because it was fading, and she always liked to sit on her porch. She walked around the property a little more than usual, but it was keeping her busy, which was doing her some good. We all knew she was missing Grandad, but she had a lot of life left in her and she needed to continue with living.

"Jasper, come give Grammy a hand, will ya?"

She went right back to hanging out with us. Grandad had been such a big part of our lives, and she did not want us to feel the great loss that it actually was for us. She figured if she had us helping her, we would realize that we had enough in her and Momma that being sad would just need to wait for another time.

Early one pleasant Saturday morning, Grammy pulled the truck to the front of the house, honked her horn, and waited for me to come out. When I did, she told me to hop in. That we were going to go for a ride. I told Momma I was heading out somewhere with Grammy, and ran out, letting the screen door slam behind me with purpose. When I got in, there was an old flannel blanket, a light brown basket, and a bottle, with what looked to be lemonade, laying in the middle between where I was seated and where Grammy was driving. There was also a small brown paper bag seated directly next to Grammy.

"What's this Grammy? Where are we going?"

"Jasper, we are going to have a picnic. It's time we have one together. Don't you agree?"

Of course, I did. I loved the time Grammy and I got to spend alone. She had spent time alone with us all, but lately, with Grandad gone now, she spent a little extra alone time with me. She knew Grandad had a lot of one-on-one time with me over the past few years, and that I desperately needed that time with him. She also knew she could not fill those shoes of his, but she would do her darndest.

We drove for about ten minutes towards town and pulled over to the side of the road. Grammy opened her door, stepped carefully out looking down the road first, and told me to get out as well. I opened the passenger door, got out, walked towards the back of the truck where Grammy was, and watched as the cars whizzed by, almost unaware of our presence.

"What are we doing now, Grammy?" I asked.

"Jasper, every picnic needs some flowers. We are going out in that field to pick us some. Any colors you want. Okay?"

I walked out and picked a few; not really understanding why I picked the ones I did. Then, I spotted some white ones that were the color of new-fallen snow and walked over to where they were. Picking those was a little harder, because they had tougher stems than the first purple ones I had grabbed. I eventually got some out and noticed Grammy had found some yellow dandelions and had them placed in a bag. I always thought dandelions were just useless weeds, but honestly, they were very pretty to look at. I walked a few more paces, grabbed a few more, and turned to Grammy to show her how good I had done picking the flowers.

She winked at me and told me we had enough for the picnic.

Back in the truck, Grammy had a blue-tinted glass vase sitting in that brown paper bag. She told me to pull the vase out of the bag and place the flowers we had just picked into it. I took the white ones out first, then added the purple. After that, I added the bright yellow dandelions, which made the flower vase look amazing. I was proud of myself, to be honest. I held it out to admire my handiwork, and Grammy glanced over as she drove.

"Why Jasper, that looks wonderful. You did a great job. I'm proud of you," as she smiled from her seat.

When we were about to enter town, Grammy made a sudden left turn. We drove along the water, down a narrow path with a hill, and over into an area away from the constant noise of town. As we got closer to the water, I saw a large wood colored cross at the entrance to a field. We drove through two large black gates opened already, and straight into the fields. There were different sized and shaped stones protruding from the ground throughout the fields. It was not an overly massive area, but it was large enough you could only see the stones at first.

When we approached the rear, a spot overlooked some of the riverbanks, blocked only by a tree line of red maples. There, Grammy slowed the truck down, pulled over onto a grassy patch, and turned off the truck. She took the key from the ignition, and sat back, looking straight ahead. I just sat there myself, unsure of where we were or what I was supposed to be doing. I still had in my hands the vase with the purple and white flowers that we had just added dandelions to for more color. Grammy stared off for a moment, then she put her head down, and asked me,

"Jasper, do you know where we are? Why we are here?"

"Umm, not really, Grammy, no I do not."

"Grandad is here" she paused. "Right over there. You see where the grass isn't fully grown yet, with the brown patches in between? In between those rose-colored stones? Right over there? That is where Grandad is. I thought today would be a good day to visit him and bring him a picnic."

I was confused. I knew he was under the green grass and dirt here in front of us, but I was not sure how we would have a picnic with him. Not knowing what to expect, I was feeling nervous and a little bit scared and my palms were drenched in sweat. I wanted to ask questions, but my mind would not get those questions to where my mouth was, to get them out in the open. I was frozen stiff for a minute, and then Grammy reached over and put her hand on mine.

"He is here in spirit, Jasper. We can't see him, but he can surely see us. I truly believe that. We are just going to have a picnic, you and me, and Grandad can look on down from up in the sky and watch over us as we do. I think he would like that Jasper, that we decided to come and visit him. He will especially like the flowers you picked out for him. Do you want to know a little secret? Grandad never sprayed the dandelions in the yard. He too, felt they were too pretty to kill. In the afternoon, he liked to sit on the porch and look over the hundreds of yellow dandelions we had in the yard. The one thing he always said to me was that it was almost as if the dandelions were singing. They always looked so firm, strong, and alive. As if they were singing straight up into the air, yearning for the sun to acknowledge them. I never understood why until this very moment. He liked the simple things. The underdog, as he would say. That man found the beauty in the weeds, as much as he did in the flowers that everyone else did. Knowing the dandelions needed so little in life to thrive and grow into that beautiful, rich yellow color fascinated him. Seeing what others could not see was something that made him special. Every living thing has just as much right to shine as another, he used to say. I didn't see that until just now, Jasper. Even with Grandad gone, he still surprises me, and I still learn from him. He was just a good, honest man."

For the first time since we arrived, tears formed in the tiny creases at the corner of Grammy's eyes. When one was ready to drop from her lids, she would wipe it clean, and then another would form in defiance, and she would continue this battle for a few moments, before she collected herself and headed over towards that bare spot in the grass. There, she laid down the old flannel blanket she had taken from the truck and smiled at the stone with Grandad's name on the front, with some dates underneath. The basket she had in her left hand, she placed gently down on the blanket, and sat down beside it.

Once she had things settled, Grammy looked over to where I was still sitting in the front of Grandad's truck, and with a gentle smile, she softly motioned for me to come over to where she was seated. I gathered myself, grabbed the flowers I had picked by the side of the road, and opened the door. As I stepped out, I could feel a strange emotion coming over me.

This was the first time I would be around my grandad since he died, and I still did not know how to feel about it all or what exactly to expect in the coming moments. I was certainly scared, but now I was feeling more sadness coming over me than anything. My mouth started to feel a slight ache a little towards the back, as if I was about to cry, but I did not want to cry. Grammy had kept from crying, so I could too, right? I was the second man of the house now, behind Davey. That was an important role, and I had to take it very seriously. Like a man should. There could be no crying, if I was a man of the house. Never had I seen Grandad cry.

He had his times where when he looked out through his dirty, cracked windshield at what seemed like a different time than the one we were in. Then he would look a little sad, but cry? Never. He was too strong for all of that. So, I thought about baseball. What Eric Davis had done the night before (he struck out twice, grounded back to the pitcher, and doubled in the eighth inning). How the Reds were looking compared to the rest of the National League. Then, I walked over to Grammy, placed the flowers down in the center of the blanket, and sat with her.

"Jasper, here. We place the flowers right on the bottom of the stone. So, everyone can see them here," Grammy explained.

"Why? Aren't they just for Grandad? How can he see them anyway? When do we know that he sees us here, Grammy? What is it we should be doing?"

Grammy just smiled, and looked over to Grandad's off-white stone, with the deep indentations that spelled out his formal name and had those dates underneath. It said,

Walter R. McFarland
Born February 26, 1917
Died May 23, 1989
May He Rest in Eternal Peace

"He knows Jasper. He knows. Let's eat. Aren't you hungry?"

As Grammy took out the food she had prepared that morning, I took out my spiral notebook, and jotted this down:

How do the people that die know we are there?
Why do we put flowers there for other people to see?
How do we know they are there?

Then I carefully and nonchalantly placed it back in my

back pocket and helped Grammy with the items she had packed. We pulled out two bologna and American cheese sandwiches that had yellow spicy mustard on them. I love spicy mustard better than regular old yellow mustard. It just tastes, I don't know really, just a little spicier, I guess. Then she had a large bag of potato chips, a jar of sliced pickles, and some napkins and paper plates. She reached over to the lemonade, opened the lid, and poured three cups. One for me, one for her, and then the third one, she poured and placed where she had just laid the flowers, at the base of the stone we were sitting next to. She knew I was watching, so without having to ask her, and without having to write that in my notebook, she just said,

"Grandad loved lemonade. So, I brought him a cup too."

For some odd reason, that made sense. Nothing else about him dying, or watching us, or the flowers so other people could see them, did. But this? It made a little sense. So, I just smiled and took a sip of my lemonade. I pictured Grandad and me sitting on the shaded front porch, looking out across the dusty road before us, to where some other time had once been, and he would tell me a story. We could talk for hours, he and I, and I never once got bored. His stories were always about a time now inevitably gone, but I could almost see what he was talking about. I felt like I could see the people he told me about, the places he once loved to visit, and the lost era he had so hoped to slow down but could not. I could almost taste the ice cream cone he had with Grammy when they first met. It was as if I were there with him, and that was my favorite part of his stories. The places he took me with just his words and facial expressions. I never felt like he was there alone.

"Grammy, do you miss him a lot? I know I sure do. I do not like that he died. Why does God let people die anyway? I mean, if he didn't let young kids die, he wouldn't need moms and dads and grandads to die. Grandad told me his mom died because she needed to help take care of all those little kids that died before she did. Why can't he just let them all live?"

She paused, wanting to explain it in a gentle way I would understand, but also in a way that she would understand as well. Grammy did not completely know what the right answer to that question was, but she tried her best to give me something that would make sense.

"Jasper, I do not know exactly why, but I know that when we die, if we are good people throughout our time here, we get to go to heaven and see all the people who died before us. When my time comes, I will get to see Grandad once again, and how great will that be! Maybe he is waiting at the gate for me, so that he can walk me in, and show me around some. When it is my time, I will surely ask God all these questions you have. If I can find a way to get you the answers, you better believe I will," and then she winked at me, making me smile and chuckle a little bit.

I sat back on my legs, took another sip, and looked at Grandad's stone. I felt the need to talk to him, so I decided to do just that. If he was there, he would hear me, and well, I had to tell him some things I never got the chance to. So, I began,

"Grandad, I didn't get to thank you. Remember all our times in town? I liked those trips, just you and me. I especially liked when you stopped by the road and told me all about when you were a little boy. All the things you got to do before, where now a building stood tall and arrogant. I liked watching you stare out and remember all those times that passed you by, because I felt like I was there with you. Thank you. I sure do miss you, but Grammy says when I die, I should be able to see you and give you a big hug. Maybe, if you are not too busy in heaven, you can wait for me at the gate too. Would that be okay? I know I will be scared, but if I see you there waiting for me, then I won't be. You always protected me, and I know you will in heaven too. Anyway, I am glad Grammy brought me here to have this picnic with you. I wish you were sitting next to me, though, but you are under the ground. But don't worry. The worms can't get you. Janet told me so and she's smart. She knows about that stuff. Tell God I said 'Hi,' and to please keep Grammy safe. I don't want to lose her too."

Grammy smiled, and said,

"Jasper, that was simply beautiful. Grandad surely is loving that we came to visit him today, and he is loving that you just told him all of what you liked. His favorite part about taking you on those rides into town, was that you liked to listen to his stories. That you asked him questions and showed a genuine interest. He liked that about you. When he would come home, he would tell me all about it, and how you would ask questions and want to learn. Grandad loved that, Jasper. Don't ever lose that. Always question things and people. It's how we learn. How we grow. I bet Grandad is smiling right now, telling his own Momma that he is proud of you and how you are growing. I bet he is doing that right now."

It made me smile, to think Grandad was walking with his Momma, talking with her, and getting to know her for the first time. I wonder if he knew who she was? She had died when he was little, so maybe someone had to point her out to him, and then he could introduce himself to her. I wanted to ask Grammy about it, but I felt like maybe I had asked a lot already. So, I wrote that one down too:

How do we know who people are in heaven that we never got to see much here on earth?

My notebook was coming in handy. The more I wrote on those blue-lined pages, the more I knew that when I got older, I would understand better. I would have all the answers I wanted, and there would be a million of them. It would take me a long time to go through all the questions I would have, but it would be worth it.

Grammy took a final bite of her sandwich, wiped the sides of her mouth with the napkin she had brought with her, and took another long sip from her lemonade glass. She looked up to the sky and squinted slightly because the sun was touching us both that morning and smiled. I watched her carefully, wondering where she was. What memory was she thinking about? So, I just imagined one of Grandad's stories where they had been walking to the movies, when they first met.

Grandad said they were holding hands, and the skies opened up over them. It rained in a sudden downpour, and Grammy was getting soaked through her clothes. So, Grandad took off his overcoat and placed it over Grammy. Only now, he was all wet! They made it to the theatre, and Grammy was laughing at Grandad being all wet. Grandad laughed along with her, and they stood there dripping and smiling at one and other. They almost missed the movie because they had forgotten what they were there for. It was, as Grandad said, his best date ever. I bet that is what Grammy is thinking about now. She's looking up to the sky and pretending like it is raining cats and dogs. She's probably smiling knowing they are laughing and dripping soaking wet to the bone and dropping water all over the carpet in the theatre. That was a good day. I was there. Well, I was there because Grandad had made it seem all so real to me. I felt I was watching them. That I could see the water running down their clothes and onto the red carpet beneath their feet. That I could smell the rain as it was on that day. That is how his stories were. They were real, and I was there with him through it all.

Chapter 10

Running from it all

* * *

After that terribly cold wintery day Momma gave birth to me, she went back to Grandad and Grammy's place to get settled in. This was just another dubious bump in the road, she thought, but man those bumps were hitting her like a freight train more and more, it would seem. Still, she had me, and with a new baby boy, Momma was all too happy to change diapers, clean spit-up, and take a few weeks off from her job and her schooling. She needed a rest. Her body and mind were getting run down, and she just needed a chance to collect herself some. Then, she figured, she could get right back to it and start her plan of getting back out on her own two feet, with her now growing family, and back to the bold dreams she had for all of us.

Grandad, though, had been keeping a close eye on Momma, because, well, she just appeared more rundown than normal. When she arrived home with her other newborn babies, she'd had more energy than a bucking bull trying to toss off a cowboy as quickly as possible. She could not sit still, and refused any help, but not in a gruff way. She just wanted to do everything for herself, and she did for the most part. Now though? She seemed a bit off. Maybe it was because she did this one alone. While she had Davey alone, she had, in some sense of the word, help through the 9 months she carried him. She had someone to return to, until she didn't, and that at least gave her hope over most of her pregnancy, until that last day. This time? There had been no man by her side for the nine months.

Grandad was there for her, but that was just not the same in her mind. She needed a companion through those lonely long pregnancy months, those nights she craved ice chips and bananas, and she had none. Maybe it was the schooling and the work finally catching up to her, while she came home and still had to attend to 3 kids, and a newborn me. He did not know for sure, but he watched her a little closer. Grammy told him it was just a part of being a mother. That sometimes after you have a certain number of children, your body and mind will inevitably go through changes. You feel different, act different, and see things differently. It would go away eventually, she assured him, and DeeBee would be back to her normal self. Laughing and energetic as ever.

Grandad agreed that it made sense, but one could tell he was not totally buying into that notion. For now, he would just be a little more present. This was important for him to do, and when he had his mind set on something, that was just how it would be. Period. You would not change that man, but he played it off well for Grammy.

I was a good baby, at least from what I was told. Not overly fussy, not really crying a lot. Mostly happier than not, and that made things a little easier for sure. Thelma Louise was a huge help to Momma, because she was the eldest, and took a liking to having a newborn baby around. It was almost as if I were a doll baby for her, and she begged Momma to change my wet diapers, and take me on small walks in the stroller Grammy had bought for Momma and me. Pushing it up the dusty road out front of the house was not an easy task, so on the days Momma went into town, Thelma Louise tagged along.

The trips to town gave her and Momma a chance to bond, as they had lost that recently. It had been some time since her and Momma enjoyed a conversation about nothing in particular, and both had missed it. Momma just figured it was a phase she was going through, and that no matter what she did for Thelma Louise, it would make no difference. Here though, with me as a new addition to the family, Thelma Louise found purpose once again. She found a reason to be around Momma more, and to actually talk with her. This extra time together was important to their fading bond, and honestly, they truly enjoyed it.

At ten years young, Thelma Louise was not what people would consider a happy go lucky child. She was moodier than not, but she did not wish to be. Her personality was one where she did not feel the need to force a candid smile, when a lot of times other people would. You know how when you are given a gift of socks and you really wanted a baseball glove, but you still forced a wide smile to be as polite and thankful as possible? She did not. Saying thank you was no issue for her. She could do that. It was the smiling she just could not draw herself to do when she did not feel like it. Momma would always just say things like,

"Oh, she's just a little tired today," or "Thelma Louise, smile honey. Are you just not feeling okay, today, honey?"

It was Momma's way of covering for her seemingly normal moody behavior that could easily come across as ungrateful, but truly, Thelma Louise did not want to feel that way. She struggled with it deep inside, and late at night, when everyone was tucked in for the evening, she would silently cry to herself until her eyes would become heavy enough to close off the world. It was just hard on her, not being able to do what everyone else seemed to do effortlessly. Why had she been feeling so down? She loved her Momma, her Grandad and Grammy. She enjoyed her siblings, although she could be found fighting with them over the simplest of things like any kids do. She did not really ask much about her birth father, having let that all stay in the past. School was okay. She had friends and did not really feel overwhelmed all that much, so she just could not put her finger on it, and it hurt her immensely. Even for a 10-year-old girl, she understood pain and frustration almost like an adult would.

It would seem that both Thelma Louise and Momma were having some changes in their moods, and energy or lack of, and even with their overall personalities. Grammy was doing her best to help with Davey, while Momma was tending to me most of the time, as the newborn baby of the family. Both Janet and Thelma Louise were attending school during the day, so that made it slightly easier on the load, but still, the dynamic of the family was changing some, and it seemed Momma was wearing thin.

Davey was finding himself in an unusual spot for him. He was the baby prior to my coming along. He was the one who got all the attention, especially from Momma. Now though? That was not the case. Watching Momma give her undivided attention, especially in those first few months of my life, was really hard for Davey. He tried doing whatever he could to get everyone's attention. First, he went back into baby mode. That is, back to fake crying, and talking like he was younger than he really was. Breaking things to get some attention was becoming the norm for him. Grammy was trying to get him under control, but Davey was having meltdowns.

One Saturday morning, Davey made up his mind to run away, and at nine in the morning, he took a duffel bag he had packed the night before, added some salted crackers for the road, and walked out the back door, down to the woods that lined the back of our house and disappeared from sight. It had just started to warm up some, but in the morning, the air still had a crisp chill to it. Davey, dressed in his favorite blue and white pajamas, with exaggerated baseballs and bats all over them, was not prepared at all. After about 30 minutes of running as far as he could, he felt as if he were far enough away that he was now "on his own." But then he felt that he heard Grandad hollering his name, over and over, coming from what seemed like slightly different directions with each shout. It was as if Grandad was calling to the left, and then to the right, and then the front of the house, and then back to the rear.

Grammy stepped off the back porch, and started to yell, "David?" then a short break of a few seconds. "Daaavvviiiddd?" This time louder.

Davey felt both accomplished and frightened. He felt like they were showing they indeed loved him, because it had not taken all that long to discover that he was missing. But what was he going to do now? And how had they been so close to him already? He had walked for a long time, at least in a five-year old's mind. Now, they were what felt like, just yards away. Davey was also feeling colder now and was hearing sounds that he did not recognize. The pajamas he had on kept getting caught on the brush in the woods, causing rips and tears and slight scratches to both his legs and arms. Maybe, maybe this was enough to show them he was serious. That he needed more attention, and that I would need less. He felt as if there was an imbalance going on, and he was protesting it in the best way he knew how. By leaving. Make everyone feel as if he were gone forever. It had taken Davey only 30 minutes or so to realize he needed to go back.

When he did head back, he could see Grandad halfway across the wooded lot, navigating the fresh growth of greens and browns. Davey put his head down and walked to him. Grandad, being the man he was, and reading situations so well, just told him,

"David, we were so worried about you! Boy, am I glad you are safe. Listen, I'll handle Grammy and your momma for you, okay? I can just tell them you needed a little walk and got lost some. That I came out to find you, and it was you that found me. Okay? Let's go back home, son. I think we could use a little ice cream in town, don't you?"

While Davey struggled with the loss of attention, Janet hardly took much notice of me at all in the beginning. She was busy being a typical 7-year-old little girl, who for some reason or another favored her left side constantly for just about everything. No one really took much notice and if they did just brushed it off as Janet being a little quirky.

This one time, when she was at another child's birthday party with friends from school, she had been holding a simple white plastic cup of apple juice in her left hand, and someone went to give her a slice of birthday cake in her right. Janet placed the cup down and almost did a complete turn so she could take the cake with her left hand, nearly knocking it to the ground in the process. The adult just thought she was being a silly kid, but Janet knew it was becoming a habit for her. She smiled slightly, almost embarrassingly, and said thank you.

The woman stared momentarily, as if she knew something was off, and later told Momma she thought something might be wrong with Janet. Momma had seen the "left hand" favoritism, but never paid much attention to it. She had once, nonchalantly, brought it up to Janet, and Janet just sheepishly nodded and tried to change the subject. Momma felt it was just a phase anyhow and not hurting anyone, including Janet, so there wasn't much of a reason to fuss. So, that was that.

As the first months turned into the first year for me, we all kind of settled into our new family life. Me without a choice in the matter, and everyone else just adjusting as families do. Life was pretty normal for the most part. Davey had stopped trying to run off, and Grandad became more of a father figure for him. Davey appreciated the bond they were forming between them, and so did Grandad. He liked that Davey would sit on the front porch steps with him and just talk. Grandad would tell Davey about the reasoning behind allowing the dandelions to grow so high, and Davey would nod and pretend to understand. Davey would tell him all about school and how his teachers were always telling him to push a little more. Try a little harder with his studies. That made Davey feel inadequate, but Grandad assured him that his time would come, and when it did, that he would do great things.

"David, every man has his time. We all get a time to shine, a time when things line up just a little more. When that time comes, you just need to be ready for it. Don't let those teachers make a fuss about too much right now. You just do the best you can son and listen to me. When that time comes, you be ready, you hear? You just be ready. The world can be yours if you are just ready," then he would look off into the distance as if he were envisioning it all for Davey.

Davey thought Grandad was giving him a speech and trying to make him feel better about how life was going at the moment. He was too young to take it to heart, but it was something he heard more than once. Just be ready when your time comes. Davey wanted to remember that, so he tried to apply it to things a little here and there. On the baseball field and waiting for a pop fly ball his way? Just be ready. Heading for a night camping in the woods with Grandad, and wondering if a bear would find its way to their food supply? Just be ready. Davey, over time, turned that into something of a personal mantra. Just be ready. One day it would be his time to shine, and he would be ready.

At Red Creek Elementary, the kids learned about many things, including Math, Science, the difference between their, there and they're, and one of the more popular subjects for young kids, their town's heritage. How did Red Creek get its name, exactly? Stories had been passed down about Indian tribes once roaming the area and that it could have been named after a chief known as Chief Red Sparrow.

When the elders of the town told the story, they sometimes chuckled at the end. Men would argue over the origin of the town name, and older men would swear by that Chief Red Sparrow legend, but the schools told a very different story of the name. In their teachings, the red in Red Creek had come from the large amount of heavy clay soil in the area. It made it nearly impossible in some areas to grow proper crops, so the Indians named it "Maxke Mpi," or Red Water. This was a Lenape Indian area, the teachers said, and they knew the land well. Well enough, to know they should plant further out, where the earth was not rich with clay. Some teachers felt that was inaccurate. That the Lenape tribe never ventured to this area at all, and that the name simply came from folklore.

Either way, as young kids growing up in Red Creek, we developed a sense of pride for our little town, and even argued like the adults did, over what we knew was the rightful reason for its name. Our parents and grandparents told us, so it must be true. The issue was that the stories were different enough, that we were really calling other people liars if we did not believe their version over our own. Boys would fistfight over the origin of a town name that ultimately meant very little. It was more about the pride of family and being right, and no Red Creek boy would let anyone tell them their ancestors were "Liars." Maybe all the bloody noses in town from those fights would become a legend as to why the town got its name one day.

Momma was feeling much better about herself, and that made Grammy, and especially Grandad happy. Maybe Grammy had been right. She just needed some time to mentally recover from her past loss and what Andy had done. Time to understand the changes that happened when you had a baby, and time to get a handle on the fact she was a single mom of four young kids. Just because she had three and they seemed to not affect her personality or mental state at all, did not mean more would not. These were things Grandad could just not understand, no matter how hard he tried. All in all, though, his DeeBee seemed back to herself, and he was quite relieved to have her. They had an incredibly strong bond, those two, and that would never change. Grandad told her it was the bond of a mighty Oak tree, and therefore unbreakable.

Yes, the McFarlands were settling back into old Red Creek Pennsylvania for the most part. Momma had changed her last name back to her maiden, and subsequently the names of Thelma Louise, Janet, and Davey too. She figured that it was time to have all the children have proper respectable last names. When a daddy left, she felt, he should take his name along with him. The kids should be proud of their names and not wonder where it had come from, or where it had gone, when someone up and left without a word. So, began the McFarland change, and the kids were feeling quite excited to share something more with Grandad and Grammy than just their home. It was exciting to have a new name. They were legitimately, McFarlands.

Chapter 11

The Series

* * *

With Grandad gone, and my list of questions growing longer by the day, life sure was different. It felt like I knew so little all the time, and I did not like that one bit. When questions would pop into my head, Grandad was sure to have the answer, and if he did not, he promised to find it for me. I had questions that he promised to find the answers to, but he never got around to it because he died before he could get me the proper answers. Dying was just stupid. I think God should wait until a man answers all the questions he had to before he can die. He should be able to take a boy for ice cream one more time and say goodbye properly. Not just die and not be able to sit on a wrought iron and plank wood bench anymore with his grandson.

When I die, I will be sure that I answer everything first. It sucks being confused and not having the right answers so I would just not be doing that. In fact, I wasn't even sure I would die anyway. Maybe I would be the first person to not die, and then I could answer everyone's questions all the time. I would just keep growing older and older, and smarter and smarter and then I would know everything and share it with the world. Even Davey.

The only problem with that, though, was that everyone around me would die. I would lose Momma one day and not be able to see her. I would want to go see Grandad and could not if I lived forever. Life was just hard, and I did not understand that all. Perhaps Grandad left because he could not find the answers and did not want to disappoint me. Maybe he left to see if God could give him the answers, and maybe he would somehow get them back to me. He was smart, so just maybe, he had died to help me with all my questions.

"Grandad, if you can hear me, it's okay. I don't need all the answers from you now. If you could just come back and have ice cream with me, that would be just great. We can talk about your stories, how something was once where something else is now. You can tell me about how you and Grammy used to dance at the hall until she was dizzy, and how she smiled and laughed when it rained on you. If you can hear this, I miss you, Grandad. I miss you a lot. So does everyone else."

Momma had gone back to her job after taking a short break when Grandad passed. She loved what she did, even if she was slightly disappointed that she was not getting further ahead. In her mind, she wanted more out of her job than to photocopy papers and put eloquently drafted letters in envelopes for other important people. She did not feel important there, even though she was as Grammy told it, "The glue that kept that dang place together half the time with some of those nitwits they have working down there."

Mr. Sheridan, the one she reported to most, had promised Momma when she started that there would be more for her to do, and that eventually, they would be expanding their offices into other areas. She would oversee greater things than she currently was, but that it would take time to get all the specifics for that. She just needed to be patient and know that better things were coming for everyone. He told her she could give her children grander things than they ever imagined. She just needed to sit tight and trust him. Things would go well, with a little patience. Momma did not have a lot of those patience things he kept talking about, but she tried.

Her children meant so much to her, and she, herself, had big plans for them. It was she that would work fingers to the bone to give us a head start. She would ensure we got the basic tools we needed to navigate the dreams she had for us. Those ties were coming, even if I did not like them one bit. Momma knew a tie was coming for me, although, I knew a Reds uniform would suit me much better.

Sadly, though, Momma had to leave her job before she had a chance to oversee greater things. Grammy sat us all down one early evening just before the horizon swallowed the light and told us Momma had to go away for a few weeks to get some things in order. It was just something she needed to do, and that when it was all handled, she would be back watching us, and working her job, fingers to the bone and all.

"Grammy, when do we get to visit with Momma?" was the first question I asked.

"Well, Jasper. Hopefully, in a few weeks there, we will be able to manage that. Your Momma knows how much she means to you all, so she just wants to get herself in a better place, and right now she is not. I reckon that once she settles in, she will be calling and setting up a time for us to visit. You will just need to be a little patient there, Jasper. I know you want to see her."

Davey seemed to take it the hardest. He did not understand why after Grandad left us, Momma needed to go too. Little seemed to bother Davey, but this, this did. Davey loved Momma and although he could be difficult at times, he just wanted her to be proud of him.

Not having a dad, he took it on himself to step up and "take care" of Momma. If she needed to do something around the house, Davey was there. In his mind, it was his job as man of the house. Now with Grandad gone, he took that to heart. He was the new man of the house, at the ripe old age of 13. I think the only thing he did not do for Momma when she asked, was to play with me. Oh, he would tell her he was gonna, but that was not always the case. Most times he just outran me or told me they were doing something that kids under the age of 10 were not allowed to do. I think he made that up, but who was I to say? What if there were events just for boys over 10 I had not heard about? Man, I cannot wait to be 10. Then he will no longer have that excuse and I can go everywhere Davey does, despite what he wants.

"So, listen up McFarlands," Grammy started up again.

"We are going to be just fine around here for the next few weeks. I will need you all to pick up more after yourselves while your momma is off getting herself straightened out. This means you are all going to help Grammy with the cooking, the cleaning and the outside work that needs tending to. Okay? We will pick up where Grandad and Momma left off, and when your momma comes back, I will be sure to tell her all about how much you helped your old Grammy. Deal?"

It wasn't so much a request, as it was a command, and while Grammy could be stern, she was also empathetic. She knew we were suffering through loss after loss, and she, for her part, would be the one consistent person in our lives. It was her way, to always be present when she was needed. Money was tight with Grandad gone, but she would still get his checks from his pension. Plus, he had earned some money from his days in the Army, and so she was getting that as well. All in all, she was going to be good, but she worried for us. The four kids that just needed to catch a break or two. Would we all get through this without a lot of life-lasting issues?

Grammy came from tough stock, but she was smart. She knew that pretending to be fine was not the same as being fine. Old people liked to talk about how hard things were when they were growing up, and just how great they were because of all those hard times. They weren't entirely incorrect. It did shape them and allow them to work much harder, save a little more, and not buy things they absolutely did not need. But at the same time, they had their share of scars. Emotional ones they did not like to talk about. The old people of Red Creek were stubborn folks. They were strongly opinionated and rarely were they able to see someone else's view as a possibility. Nope, you either agreed with them or you were a...

I remembered where I heard my name now! Jasper! The old men had called anyone who did not agree with their views Jaspers. Why on earth had Grammy called me a name that meant I was wrong, or did not agree with them? Was Davey right? Did she name me after stubborn old men who were stupid? I was feeling a warm trickle inside. Anger, but sadness as well. I loved my nickname Grammy gave to me, but not if it meant I was just a dumb, stubborn old man. This was something I wanted to ask Grammy, but with all that was going on, it would need to go into the notebook until later. Once she had settled down and Momma was home, though, I would confront her and ask for sure.

"Jasper. Grammy, why did you name me after some dumb old men who never agreed with anything anyone else said? Do you not think I am smart?"

The entry was made, so for now, as best I could anyway, I would let it go until later. But it would get asked. That I was sure of.

That October, Eric Davis was playing in Game One of the World Series, and they were facing the mighty, repeating World Series Champs, the Oakland A's. No one expected the Reds to even be there, and honestly, I was worried. The

A's had all the big names. Mark McGuire. Jose Canseco, Walt Weiss, and a pitcher named Dave Stewart. However, The Reds were fighters. Just like the boys from Red Creek were. When Eric Davis took Dave Stewart deep in the first inning, and it cleared the fence, both Davey and I jumped off the ground and danced and shouted.

Davey was not as big of a Reds fan as I was, but he did not want Oakland to win. Oakland was supposed to win. They were the team no one wanted to play, and they had the best players, playing for the best team. The Reds were good, but severe underdogs. Just like Grandad said about those dandelions, though, root for the underdogs. He would have loved this series had he been alive still to watch it. Maybe he was sitting up with his Momma, watching way down here, as the Reds got hit after hit against the great Dave Stewart.

Davey was so ecstatic to have new excitement in his life at that moment, that he even high fived me! Me, his little annoying brother who always tried to tag along, he actually gave a high five to! He saw the shocked look on my face, and just smirked slyly. He knew it meant the world to me, and even had he done it out of pure excitement and not to be extra nice to me, he wasn't about to take that back. No way, no how. Grammy even got in on the action.

"Well, David and Jasper, that looks like a good start for the Reds huh?" She was smiling. Not because she liked baseball. She did not care for sports at all. No, she smiled because for the first time in a while, her boys were genuinely enthusiastic about something. This was making her just tickled with her own excitement, and she looked up and quietly begged God for the Reds to win this one game. Just to give her grandsons this one night of victory, and off from the inner turmoil they had been fighting. It would mean so much, she thought. So, she prayed and then said a quick hello to Grandad.

When the game went on, and the Reds piled on the hits and the runs, we just grew more and more electrified. The whole town could hear us, we thought, as we screamed and shouted at the television. By this time, both Janet and Thelma Louise had scampered down to see what all the commotion was. They saw Davey and I high fiving after each hit. We even managed something that resembled a hug at one point, and Grammy was just sitting there soaking it all in. The sisters looked at Grammy confused, and she just winked at them and motioned for them to have a seat. They sat down, watching us go crazy over what was happening on that tiny TV, wondering how we were able to follow along. It was the Reds. The Cincinnati Reds! Who didn't know who the Reds were? Who hadn't heard of Eric Davis? He was only the best player in the National League, well, to me he was. In fact, I felt he was the best player in all of baseball, both leagues included. He had already hit for the cycle last year, and now, now he had the chance to help beat the giant Oakland A's.

The girls laughed at how excited I was, and how Davey was actually reacting to my excitement. He had never ever been excited when I was, but now? This was new unchartered territory. What happened that night was almost a miracle, I felt. Grammy, Janet, Thelma Louise, Davey, and Me. All watching baseball. All getting along, and no one fighting or complaining about this or that. No sir. We were all living in this very monumental moment. We were all dandelions that night, singing high into the sky, over my team. My player. This was my night, and I was thrilled beyond any doubt to be sharing that with the people I loved most. For a night, nothing else mattered. I missed Momma but knew she would be back when she was ready. I missed Grandad something terrible, but he would be cheering along in heaven watching this game and rooting for the Reds as we all were now.

Over the next three games, it became a ritual for all five of us to converge in that living room, sitting exactly where we had that first night, and just watch. I was being very superstitious and trying hard to not change the course of anything, so I sat in the very same Indian style position I had during that first victory.

Game two was a much closer game than the first, the Reds won in 10 nail-biting innings. Both Janet and Thelma Louise were covering their eyes, afraid to see what was going on. It was nerve-racking and they, despite knowing nothing about the game, were quite nervous. Probably more so for me, knowing how much I cared about the outcome. I was not as excited going into the later innings, but when the 10th came and Joe Oliver singled in the winning run, I screamed and just about lost my voice. It was mayhem in that living room. Everyone was hugging wildly and high fiving and laughing contagiously. Nothing was better.

The third game was more like the first, with the Reds dominating and winning by a score of 8-3. At the very end of that game, Thelma Louise asked just how many they had to win to be called "The Champs."

"One more, Thelma Louise. One more! Can you believe it? If we win just one more game, we beat the A's and we will be the champions of Baseball!"

She saw my excitement and said,

"Ronnie, I can feel it. I can feel a victory coming. So, you get ready to celebrate, okay?"

I was smiling from ear to ear because Thelma Louise was smart. A lot smarter than me and Davey were. Maybe even smarter than Janet, although she was pretty smart herself. She had to know something, to ensure a victory for my Reds. I just stood there, taller than before. Feeling proud, almost as if I were playing in the championship games myself. Each time Eric Davis came to the plate, I pretended like I was the one in the batter's box. I was seeing the pitches come in lightning fast just as Eric Davis would. I was swinging the bat when he was swinging the bat. When he hit a home run, I was the one circling the bases, pumping my fist high into the air.

It was just a matter of time before I was big, and playing for the Reds myself, I figured. Momma wanted me to succeed, and that sounded like a pretty successful job. I would circle the bases, playing for the Cincinnati Reds, and Momma would be in the stands watching me, telling everyone within earshot, "That's my boy." She would be smiling and waving, and I would wave back to her and she would be happy and proud. I just needed to practice a little more and get a little bigger first.

Before the start of game four, I washed up, and brushed my teeth, so I could sit and enjoy the night without having to worry about dumb grooming chores after the game. Nothing would interfere with the moment if the Reds pulled off the impossible feat of sweeping the Oakland A's. Nothing.

When I walked into the living room and made my way to my "spot," there was a medium-sized box laying on the floor before me. Davey was already at his seat, a chair to the right of the room. Grammy was in her spot, and both Thelma Louise and Janet were seated on the left side of the couch, next to Grammy.

"What's this? What is in the box?" I asked, dumbfounded.

"Open it," Davey said before giving anyone else a chance to utter a word. He seemed overly excited for a box, more than I've ever seen from him, so I did not know what to expect.

I sat down gently on the floor, looked over at Grammy, and she winked. Then I looked over to my sisters, and both were looking at each other, smiling and giggling like little kids. The box was an old Christmas present box Grammy had saved from last Christmas. I knew because the tape had ripped some of the brown packaging when I had opened it last year to reveal a gold striped sweater my Aunt had bought me that I hated. It was taped again, but in different spots. So, I tore gently at the tape, trying to be careful so Grammy could reuse it for a third time.

"Oh, Jasper, don't worry about that old box. Rip her open! I want to see what's inside!" Grammy said smiling.

I pulled hard at the sides, breaking the hold that the tape had on the box, and pulled off the top. There was a white piece of tissue paper laid on the top, so I pulled at that and set it aside next to the top of the box I had pulled off. When I looked back at the box, there, staring back at me, was an ivory-colored shirt, with dark Red letters and numbers printed on to it. My eyes got so big, I thought they may pop out of my head. This was not just a shirt. This was a jersey. When I pulled it all the way out from its temporary home, it revealed what I had only dreamed of. On the back was the number 44 shining perfectly in the dim light, and above that was just one name. Davis. It was an Eric Davis Jersey, and I was now holding it in both my shaking hands, high above my head.

"Whose jersey is this? Where? Where did, I mean, is this mine?" I said, trying to form a complete sentence through all my confusion and excitement.

"It's for you, dummy, I mean, Ronnie. We all thought that this would be the perfect gift for you for tonight. Especially when those Reds win. Don't ya think?" Davey answered.

I stared and did not know what to say. This was the best gift I had ever received. No one had ever given me an Eric Davis Jersey to wear. And for the final game of the World Series? No way the Reds were losing now. Not with this family all pulling for them. Not with this Jersey I was now putting on over my Pajamas. It was just a matter of getting through the next nine innings, and I could proudly wear my Jersey at school and around town for everyone to see. I was with the winners.

"Jasper, I went into town and well, a man had some sports stuff in his store window. I stopped in and told him who your favorite player was and asked if he had anything with that young ballplayers' name on it. He showed me this, and although it's a little big, well, you can grow into it and have it for a long, long time. Your sisters and David knew you would love it. I just couldn't leave that man's store without getting that jersey for you. So, think of it as an early Christmas present. It's yours to keep."

Nothing. Nothing could make this night bad. Not even a Reds loss. However, it did not matter. In another razor-close game, the Cincinnati Reds pulled it off. They beat the mighty Oakland A's in four straight games. No one could have ever predicted it, but those Reds were fighters. They knew how to win, and how to fight the much bigger, stronger opponent. Oakland had power, but they did not have the heart of the underdogs. They did not have the same faithful fans the Reds did, cheering from miles away, with each hit, each pitch, praying for a victory. They did not have an eight-year-old boy, wearing a number 44 jersey, sitting in an old faintly lit living room, with the best people around. That was the difference I told myself. The Reds had become world series champs, and we had helped. I could go to sleep happy, feeling like a winner, for the first time in a long time.

Now all I needed was my momma home, and all would be right in the world.

Chapter 12

Counting Plates

* * *

"Put on your tie Jasper," is all I kept hearing all morning. "We are leaving soon to visit your momma," Grammy was telling me.

I knew we were seeing Momma, but still, I did not want to wear a stupid tie again. I wore one when Grandad died, and now I had to wear a tie all over again? Why? It made no sense. Momma did not care if I had a tie on. She just would be glad to see me. But Grammy insisted, so I wore the dumb tie. I was trying to figure out this letter I wanted to write. It had been several months now since we had seen our Momma, and that was only supposed to be for a few weeks. So much had been going on that Momma missed, and I wanted to write about that. I wanted to write about the year since Grandad had passed. Still, I had a lot of trouble with addressing it, so I skipped the name part for now, and went to the writing of the actual letter. I would need to come back to that though because it was getting to be time to head to Momma's car she had left behind. It was the only way for us all to have seats and travel safely. Grammy had Grandad's old pickup truck, and although she would still let us sit in the bed of that truck on short trips into town, this was not one of those times.

When we all piled in, Davey was pretty quiet. It was not like him to just sit in silence, but he was, and I just let him be. We had not experienced the Reds winning the series yet. That magical night where we finally connected. Seeing Momma was a few months before our time of high fiving, so I was still treading lightly with Davey. Janet seemed happy, but then again, she always seemed happy. I know she missed seeing Momma around the house, but she always hid how she felt more than the rest of us. I couldn't hide my excitement ever. Davey wore his heart on his sleeve as well, but certainly not Janet. She was a cool cucumber and always making the peace whenever she had the chance.

Thelma Louise, well, she was down. She talked very quietly with Grammy in the front seat. I could not hear from the back seat of the car. Partially because Momma's car was loud and probably needed a new muffler any day now, but also because Grammy and Thelma Louise did not want us to hear their conversation. It was theirs, so I figured it was none of my business. I saw Davey straining to hear. He would slide up in his seat a little at a time, so as to not be noticed. No one seemed to notice, or maybe they did, and they did not care. I'm not sure if he heard anything, but if he did, it did not improve his mood one bit.

The ride was much longer than our rides into town. We had to cross over the Ohio border, and so Grammy told us to just relax and look out the window and enjoy the nature God had provided for us. There wasn't much to see in my opinion, other than trees and some mountains along the way. Janet came up with an idea, and I thought it was great. We would see how many different state license plates we would find on the way there, and then how many we could find on the way back. Davey was not interested in playing, and so Janet and I started. Of course, Pennsylvania was the easiest. We were still in the state, so that one would be on both lists we had made. Janet wrote them in the journal she was carrying with her, and I was looking as closely to each car as I could. I discovered that the big trucks, the 18 wheelers, as Grammy called them, had mostly all out of State plates. The first one I saw was Wisconsin and so I shouted that to Janet,

"Janet, look Wisconsin!"

"Ronnie good one! Keep looking, Ronnie. Let's see how many we can find!" she said.

Davey was just sitting there, his elbows on his knees and his head propped in his hands, and I did not know what to make of it. Why did he not want to play with us? This was a good way to pass the time, but he had no interest whatsoever. We were also, more importantly, going to be seeing Momma for the first time in a very long time, and here he was, sulking. Still, he clearly was trying to listen to what Grammy was talking about with Thelma Louise, and so again, I just let him be.

"Ronnie, look, Vermont! That is a good one, Ronnie. It's the other way so they must be traveling like us."

Wow, who would have thought there were so many different states with so many uniquely colored license plates? This was a lot more fun than I thought it would be. Who knows? Maybe we would find them all if we drove long enough and kept going all the way through Ohio.

"Janet, how many different license plates are there?" I asked.

"Well, Ronnie, there are enough for each state, and then some from other countries too. I don't expect to see any of those, but we may see a lot of the state ones. Do you know how many states there are, Ronnie?" she asked.

"No, he does not. He has no idea of how many states there are. Do you, Ronnie?" Davey said in his sarcastic voice.

"Ignore him, Ronnie, it's okay. There are 50. 50 states, Ronnie. They will teach you about them all in school soon, Ronnie," Janet calmly said back as she shot a quick glare towards Davey.

Wow. I could not believe it. Fifty States? That was a lot. More than I had even thought. My guess would have been maybe around twelve or something more like that, but I was not going to tell them that now. I knew how many there were after Janet told me, so I just pretended I did know, and went back to searching for more plates. Every few minutes, for the first half-hour, we were finding new states, and Janet was writing them down, one at a time. She was letting me find most of them, so she could write and focus on that. We found Ohio, Tennessee, Virginia and Maryland. Then came Illinois and Texas, and right behind that on one of them big 18 wheelers, came Montana. I had never heard of Montana, so that one was fun for me. There were no baseball teams there in Montana. Maybe that is the reason I had never heard of it. Either way, it was on a t massive truck we passed by, so it must be a state. By the time we got over the border, and into Ohio, we were getting a little restless. It had been a while since we were on a trip like this, and my legs were growing numb. Plus, I had to pee.

"Grammy, are we close? I really have to go pee," I said.

She just kept driving on and did not answer me back. I was unsure if she heard me over the noise of the muffler, but not wanting to bother her, I just waited and held it in as best I could, squeezing my hands between my legs that were already pressed together tightly. Janet looked over and told me it could not be much further. We had to be getting close, she figured. I mean, really. How big could Ohio be? I knew the Reds played there but did not know much else. It was flat. Real flat, driving on that road. Sometimes, we would hit a bump, and I could feel my bladder dancing inside me like a Mexican jumping bean. Finally, I could take no more.

"Grammy? I think I am going to pee my pants. I really gotta go."

Davey yelled that I better not pee in the car, and finally, Grammy took the car, reared it off to the shoulder, and brought it to a complete stop.

"I need to stretch my legs," Grammy began. You all should get out and stretch. We are almost there, but it's good to get that blood flowing some. Jasper, you can go over into those there weeds and pee. No one will see you. The cars are going way too fast to even be bothered by us here," she finished.

Davey made a joke about how no one wanted to see me anyway, and Grammy told him to hush his mouth. He did.

I walked over to the edge of the road, found a cleared spot where I could take a few steps in, away from the shoulder we had pulled over on, and looked around. All I saw was some soda cans laying around in the weeds, some crumpled up newspapers caught by the tall grass, and a million cigarette butts scattered throughout. I guess peeing on those would do nothing. I imagined they were all lit, and sprayed my pee all over the ground, putting each out as I sprayed. My mind was always searching for something out of nothing.

When I had finished, at least in my mind, extinguishing all the fires, I zipped my pants back up, looked out for a second at the field and wondered, what would be there when I grew up. Would it be a field still, as it was now? Untouched, pure, innocent? Or would some big company come in and build a large brick building that people with ties and fancy dresses would work in? Grandad always had me thinking about that kind of stuff. What he saw once, and what he saw later, were entirely different pictures and it bothered him some. Would this bother me if something were built all the way out here on the side of some road in Ohio? Perhaps, I figured. Perhaps. But I had only a moment to think because Janet was calling me back to the car, telling me we were about to leave once again, with or without me. So, I scampered back over the weeds and shoulder, into the back seat once again, and off we were on our way, heading to see Momma.

Back on the road, Grammy began to talk.

"Listen up McFarlands. When we get there, you stay with Grammy, you hear? Your Momma will be in a room on the third floor, but there are a lot of people there, and, well, it's better you just stick with me, okay? Also, Momma is, Momma is going to be sleepy. She has to take her medications, and because of that, she sleeps a lot. So, it's okay to hug her and talk to her, but she may not be very talkative. Just until, you know, she comes home."

Davey asked, "Grammy, is she coming home soon?"

"I do not know, David. I really am not sure. I know she wants to come home, just as soon as she is well enough, but she needs time. Momma wants to be back to her very best self, so that when she comes home, she will be able to take care of you like a momma should. So, it may be some more time, but know that she is working towards that day, alright David?"

Davey crouched back into his seat and said nothing. He was not happy with that answer, and so I was not either. My concept of time was different than his, and I truly felt Momma was coming home in a few days. Davey, he had felt it may be a lot longer, if ever. This bothered him, and scared him, and me. Janet saw Davey was feeling down, and just put her left arm around him, and whispered something into his ear, pulled away slightly, still looking at him, and smiled. He did not seem to notice, nor did he move. Whatever she had said did not help, but at least she was trying. Janet looked over to where I was and smiled warmly. I smiled a little back, but I was now feeling like I just wanted to cry instead of smile. My eyes were getting the watery feel to them, and I was having trouble seeing without things being blurry. Janet told me to look out for more license plates, but I couldn't see well now. Everything was just a blurry mess as I tried to hold those warm tears back. Pretending as if I were looking out the dirty window once again, I fooled Janet. Or at least I think I did.

When we veered off the highway, Grammy drove down a long windy road. There were no houses in sight. Just overgrown evergreen trees for as far as I could see. The road was wide at first, but then closed in, almost as if it were one lane towards the end. At the top of the road, just beyond all those evergreen trees we had passed, stood a large black gate with fancy lettering on the top. I could not read it but knew Janet could tell me later on what the words were. There stood a man in uniform at the entrance to the gate, and he motioned for us to drive over to him. The gate already appeared to be half-opened, but maybe it was because it would not shut. It was old, the paint fading and chipping away, and looked like it could fall at any time now.

"Ma'am," the man began. "How can I help you?"

"Hi, we are here to see Dolores McFarland. We have an appointment already in place," Grammy responded kindly but trying to sound as professional as she could.

The man was looking right at Grammy, and then he

paned his eyes around the car, looking at each of us closely, then back to Grammy.

"These all her kids, Ma'am?"

"Yes," she replied. "We are all here to see her. The kids and me. They have not seen her in some time, and it's been a long drive, so if you do not mind, we would like to get on in there," she said, this time, a little more sternly and impatient.

The man in the uniform jotted something down on his board he held in his hand, took out his walkie talky, and spoke into it:

"Five coming in. One woman, and four little kids. All five to see Dolores McFarland."

After a few seconds, a scratchy voice came back to this man and told him to send them on through.

"Roger that," the man replied.

"Okay, Ma'am. You are going to drive through the gate, and veer left as you get to the fountain. From there you will park in the lot marked "A," and then a man will meet you at the entrance closest to the lot. He can take you to see Dolores, and ensure you are all safe."

As the gate opened, I grew nervous. What did he mean, ensure we were safe? Why would we not be safe? It was only Momma we were here to see. I did not like how the man said that and grew even more nervous. My stomach got those knots you get when you are anxious, chasing a flyball, and my throat felt as if it were closing in on me. Maybe I should have waited until Momma was back home to see her.

Chapter 13

Without Momma

* * *

It's funny, looking back on the things that shape you, mold you into just the person you are to become. All the events we witness and go through firsthand in our past are destined to shape the person we become in our future. Some people take hardships and tragedy as a sign of weakness and failure. Some, as a valuable lesson to learn what not to do when new and difficult situations arise. It is all a part of balance, and what we McFarlands did was try to balance every lesson, for better or for worse.

Sometimes we'd plow right through them and take them as valuable lessons indeed, and sometimes we'd fumble and fall backwards, losing ground and stumbling slightly in a direction not where we intended to go. There was no blueprint for how we reacted to every event we faced, and the challenges were welcomed head-on, or cursed about because, why us? Things that seemed easy enough to overlook were sometimes the hardest to.

In middle school, I started to find myself and learned

where I had talent and excelled, and where I needed to work a little harder. Technically, I was still small for my age, but I hit a growth spurt, and I took notice. So did Grammy. She would tell me I was going to eat her out of house and home if I continued to grow, but she always said it with a wink. It was something unexpected, but something she welcomed. I had a hard time in school with being bullied for not having a dad, not having the best sneakers, and well, just because they could. Bigger kids always seemed to pick on the smaller weaker ones, and I was one.

It didn't make it any easier after Momma went away. In the beginning we expected her back at any moment, but as time continued to move on, it became apparent she needed a lot more help than her living on the outside with us would provide for her. Time just went on.

That day we first visited her was so difficult, and I remembered, looking back on it, just how much I cried. She was simply not the Momma that had left, and not the one I remembered hugging me when I was really little and all I needed was a warm hold. The woman we saw was different. She was sad but tried to put on her best happy face. She was confused, and clearly on a high dosage of medication. When Grammy saw her, she broke down and had to quickly leave the room. My Grammy, who was a tough SOB, just could not handle the sight of her little girl, all alone and away from her family, struggling to get better while clearly looking the worse. She composed herself long enough to come back in and spend some time with Momma, but it was just not the same. Grammy was never one to hold her tongue, but she had so much trouble just talking. It was as if she did not even know the woman in front of her. She was straining to just understand.

Momma had lost weight, and that was scary because she was never a bigger woman to begin with. She could have only weighed 120 lbs. before she went away, and now, Grammy felt she had gone down to maybe 90 at the most. It was hard, seeing our Momma like that, in a place full of people roaming the shallow halls in white jackets, white pants, and black shoes. They were telling people, with force behind their words, what to do. How to walk. Asking over and over "Where do you think you are going? Isn't it time for your meds? Jeremiah, you can't skip your meds tonight, so do not play me like that again, you hear?"

It was just the worst, scariest place for an 8-year-old to be, and then it hit me. This is where my momma was living now. While I was complaining about playing baseball with Davey and his friends teasing me nonstop about anything and everything, my momma was in this place, being told what to do, when to do it, and how. She was being fed medication that seemed to deplete her of all her energy. This woman who had struggled through raising four young children, with fathers who either were not present, or unable to be present, and who had put herself through school while working a full-time job and sometimes adding a part-time one to that, was now losing not only all that she had worked for, but her very self. Her identity was lost among the bare white walls and rusted metal clad windows this massive faded red brick building had.

Nothing was warm about her new home, and I hated that for her. She was used to small areas she made uniquely comfortable for her and us. Now, she had no warmth. No wall hangings around with pretty flower landscapes or multicolored quilts laying over tan couches to add just enough color to make one smile. No. She had white walls. Ugly green tiled floors that were chipped more than not. She had these men and women barking at everyone, scaring them into submission, and I wanted to just go. Now.

Grammy looked around at the surroundings and you could see for the first time, she was scared. I do not think she liked this place for Momma at all, but she never let on.

"Dolores? Hey. It's Mom. Hi honey. DeeBee, can you hear me?" Grammy asked.

There was no response. Momma just looked down at her own feet, as if trying to figure out how those blue socks had gotten to where they were. She shifted back and forth ever so slightly, but enough you could notice it. Her hair was up and appeared to have been cut much shorter. Her warm smile was gone, and she had a slight white film at the corner of her mouth. Her big brown eyes were more pupil than brown, and her skin looked milky, and almost as if it had a shine to it. She did not look good, but the woman in the room with us assured Grammy that things were working for Momma. She was progressing better and responding to the medications as anticipated. This was a great start, she told Grammy.

I did not like that woman. She was big and had a mole right on the top of her lip. Her hair was short and full of curls. One of those perms that I saw people getting in town when we stopped for ice cream. Her teeth were yellowed and had black marks on the sides. When she looked at me and smiled, I turned away and put my head into Janet's lap. Janet took her hands and placed them gently on top of my head, and just stroked my hair back and forth lightly.

My eyes were filling with tears and I remembered Grammy telling me on the way there, that we needed to be strong for Momma because she would want that, so I just dug deep down inside and told those tears they would just need to wait. Seeing Grammy cry at first was probably more than Momma needed already, so I was not going to be adding to that. No sir. I was the second man of the house behind Davey, and men of the house did not cry. They fixed things. That was my plan. I would fix Momma, and she would be right as the sun again. Then she could come back home, live with Grammy and all of us, and life would just go back to the way it was, without Grandad, of course. That one, I realized, I would not be able to fix. Even if it was what I wanted.

When my 8th Grade graduation came, I was feeling both nervous and proud. Here I was, a runt of a boy, growing more each day though, and about to head into the unpre-dictable world of high school. Davey had graduated the year before from the same high school and was now off to Western Calico Regional College. He had a partial scholar-ship for baseball, and although he was not starting, he was getting some playing time. Grammy had taken me to a game of his, that was about 3 hours south of where we lived, and I saw him sitting in the dugout, cheering his team on. He did not get to play in that game, but just seeing Davey in a sharp uniform, just like Eric Davis was wearing, was awesome. Grammy was a little sad he did not get to play, but I reminded her how great it was that we got to see him all dressed up, and that it was not in a suit and tie.

"See Grammy, he doesn't need a tie to look sharp! He has cleats on his feet, and a fresh uniform. Just wait, Grammy. One day I will have that on too, and Davey and I will be big league ballplayers. You will be proud and attend all our games, cheering us from the stands. Won't that be great, Grammy? Momma will be home by then, I suppose. She can come along too!"

Grammy would just give me that smile and wink as she often did, and that was enough. I knew she loved how my imagination and determination had gotten me so far. Davey had changed over time. We still had our share of fighting, but as he grew older, things shifted for him. He met new friends and started dating. Baseball had become more of a job than a pleasure for him. He needed to memorize signs now, whereas before he would simply read the pitcher and just steal a base. He had to work for hours upon hours on basic hitting drills and chase shallow flyballs over and over and over again, until his glove was worn out. Even worse, he had to suffer through watching his teammates play the game he loved while he rode the bench, and he had to accept that. Never in his glorious high school days had he sat on the bench. Nope. He was a star at his school, and when he came to bat, people dropped everything and watched.

He didn't have immense power, but he had an instinct that allowed him to find the holes where players were not. When he connected his bat to a baseball, you could nearly hear and feel the heart he had. He would drill that ball as hard as possible through the openings and without a blink of his eye be off to base. He was fast too, so many times what would be a single for most players would turn into a double, and a double into a triple.

I was proud of Davey but wondered what high school would have in store for me. He had been out of school for just a year, but here came the younger McFarland boy. Would people wonder? What would he do? Could he play ball like his older, much more popular brother? What if I tried out for the team, and embarrassed myself? I was under so much pressure to be like Davey, that my head was spinning. That summer would be so hard on me. I would really need to think about what I expected of myself, and just how much I would be able to push myself, or I would fail. Plain as day.

Grammy and I became even closer once Davey left for school. Janet left for college two years before Davey, but she headed out west instead. Her destination was a small town in Washington called Winthrop, to a school that specialized in Engineering. She had always been good at solving issues, so engineering was a perfect fit for her. When she left, I cried. Janet was my rock. She was the one that always knew how to cheer me up, or how to make me laugh.

She promised to call often, and initially, she had kept that promise. But as time went on, and her school workload combined with her part-time job she needed to help with her classes took precedence, I heard from her less. I would be lucky if I heard from her once a week after the first year she was away and began to not expect her calls much at all. Grammy told me that Janet was just working so hard, so she could become a big shot engineer, designing things for big firms, or even NASA maybe, she said. Imagine that. My sister Janet, who was from this unimportant tiny town of Red Creek, Pennsylvania, might be working on the space shuttle one day. I could tell everyone in town how my older sister was sending those big shuttles up to the moon. No one else in town could claim that.

Things did not go the same for Thelma Louise. She did not take the route of going to college to further her education. Instead, she had married a man named Michael Garbrant, who was a star football player at Red Creek High. Michael had started off by going to college, but he did not last long. Mainly because Mike did not take well to people telling him what to do.

In high school, he ran the show, calling his own plays, and basically getting away with whatever he wanted. In his senior year, he was caught stealing liquor from a store in town, and when the police went to press charges, the town went into an uproar. Their star player could not be shamed like this over such a silly stunt. He was just fooling around, they reasoned. Nothing serious and no one was hurt. No harm, no foul they said. So, Mike just continued to believe he was invincible, even at the college level.

He quickly found out that a star player for Red Creek

High, was not a star player at the college level. Mike didn't amount to much, but Thelma Louise loved him, and they had 2 children, Patrick Michael and Natalie Rose. I loved playing with them when they came to see Grammy. Mike wound up working for Oliver's Groceries in the deli department, and Thelma Louise at the same diner that Momma worked at when she had me. As soon as the owners knew who she was, they hired her on the spot. Momma was loved at that place.

Thelma Louise did not talk much at all about Momma. When the owners asked how she was doing, she would just say she was doing okay, and had been away working on some things. The owners knew, and so did most everyone in town, that Momma had been away for a good long time. They called it a nervous breakdown, but I never knew Momma to be nervous much. I think she just needed a break from all the running around she was always doing, but I was getting the feeling that she would not be coming home. It hurt us all, but Thelma Louise took it a little deeper herself. I think she felt that being moody when she had, and making a fuss out of nothing growing up, had sent Momma into that nervous breakdown the town people had been referring to. I did not think it was her fault, but it seemed she still felt like she should take some of the blame.

Momma had not seen her two grandchildren yet. Mike thought that where Momma lived was not a place for kids to be, and I had to agree. Remembering back to when Grammy had driven us there those years back, it was not a good experience at all. Those people screaming and crying in the halls, falling on the floor, and drooling all over themselves. It was like a horror show to that younger me, and I could not wait to get out of there. Can you imagine if two little kids, smaller and younger than I was then, went there to visit Momma and saw what I saw? It would scar them for life.

Grammy said I was exaggerating a bit, but I know what I saw, and I remember having bad dreams when we got back home. That was not how I wanted to spend my sleeps. Waking and seeing people over top of me, drooling all over my blankets as I tried to move. I could not get out of bed because of fear, and when I awoke, my body felt stiff as a board with my heart racing in a frantic matter. Those were the worse nights I can remember having. Worse than just missing Momma, was imagining the place where she had to live.

Momma had not improved much at all, and Grammy, who was getting older, was growing more and more worried about what would happen if she passed. I did not want to think about that, because Grammy had raised me for so many years on her own, and without her, I thought I would be lost. She was always saying things like,

"Jasper. I am getting old, son. Listen to me. If anything should happen to old Grammy, you be sure to always stay in touch with your brother and sisters, you hear? You keep in touch with your momma. She's going to pull out of this one of these days. I can just feel it. When she does, she will need family, and you will be all the family she has left. When I go, if your momma is not well enough yet, I will tell God he needs to speed that up, so she gets herself all good. Life is not slowing down, and she has a lot of life left in her bones to live. He will need to understand that when old Grammy tells it to Him that way."

I never understood when she talked about God. How was it we prayed to Him for things, but that she still felt she needed to see Him in person to make a better argument? At night she made us all say prayers, and I always prayed for my momma to come home. Only, He was not listening well enough. I know He was busy and all, but He had to hear me eventually I thought. Only, He had not. For that, I was angry. It didn't matter, though. I still said my prayers every night. I figured if I missed one night, and that just so happened to be the night He was listening, I may miss the opportunity to get Momma home, and I was not willing to take that chance.

I spoke to Grandad a lot as well. Mainly asking for the same thing. To send Momma home. Put in a good word with God and see if he could swing it. After all, everyone here loved Grandad so I imagined it would be the same in heaven. He was good with people, so I am certain as soon as he walked through the front door, he was meeting people, and impressing them with his stories. Maybe he was even pointing down telling them what once stood where there were office buildings now. They would be impressed he remembered that all. I also asked him to not need Grammy soon. I remember he told me sometimes mommas died so they could take care of the little kids that had died before them, and I did not want him to need Grammy yet. I wanted her to stay for a long while, because if she were gone, who would take care of me? I could not raise myself yet. There were bills to pay and groceries to buy. I could barely make eggs in the morning. I would starve, I thought to myself.

Freshman year would be a tough one. I just figured I would do the best I could, and if people asked me about my brother, I would tell them how great he was doing playing ball in college. That he would be playing pro ball in no time and put in a good word for me.

That's how it worked. There are tons of brothers and father/sons who play major league baseball. We could do it if they could. So what if my brother wasn't getting much playtime and riding the bench? He was going to play more next year, he figured, so then he could prove himself and that is when things would change for the McFarland Brothers. I would play right field and he would play left. We would throw runners out trying to head home and people would fear us. The dynamic duo playing outfield for the Reds. Hopefully, Eric Davis was still playing. He could show us the ropes. How to be famous, and sign autographs. All famous ball players do that. They sign autographs. I've never seen a ballplayer up close, but if I did, I would ask for his autograph and tell him one day I would be signing cards too. That he may want to get my autograph now before I got famous and became harder to get to. Eric Davis was famous. He won the World Series when I was just 8 years old. I never forgot that night. It was the best night of my life.

Grammy was going to be 78, and so I told Davey to

hurry it up. By the time I got to the big leagues, she would be maybe a hundred. She needed to watch Davey play a game so she could imagine what it was like if she went blind when I was playing. Davey said I was acting a fool, but I was serious! It could happen. Besides, Grammy was always telling the old folks in town about how her grandchildren were doing such great things. She loved talking about us, even Thelma Louise. Grammy swore she had Momma's fight in her, and that she would find her way eventually and get life going in the right direction. Just as soon as she left that no good fool Michael. She did not like Michael. Grammy had a good sense for people, and Michael rubbed her the wrong way, constantly. When he stopped over with Thelma Louise and the kids, he would say something like,

"Hey! Hey, Grammy. How's it going? Fighting off any squirrels lately?"

He never made any sense to me, and Grammy disliked when other people called her that. She reserved that very important title for her grandchildren only, and he was not one of us. No sir, he was not even close. If Grandad were alive, he would punch Mike in the face for calling Grammy, Grammy. That I know for certain. Grandad was tough and no star football player from Red Creek High would be a match for him. I do not know honestly what Thelma Louise saw in him, but she seemed happy, I guess. Not head over heels, as Momma used to always say people were, but okay with it. She might have made her decisions quickly at times, but she stuck by those decisions just the same.

I just wanted to get things moving. The unknowns of

starting high school and all that went with that was causing me to have panic attacks. Not really, but they sure felt like attacks, if I knew what those felt like, which I did not. My friend's momma would get them all the time and he would tell me about it. She would just scream and cry and shut down, and he would leave out the backdoor and head over to our place until he thought she had calmed down enough. It became a regular thing for Grammy to see him at our house. She did not mind, though, having another boy over. It reminded her of me and Davey being there, and she missed that. Besides, he was a good kid, Zach. He just had a momma who was not right sometimes, so Grammy welcomed him with open arms, and plenty of her buttered biscuits.

Chapter 14

The Change

* * *

Tryouts for the Red Creek High freshman squad were just days away, so I continued to play ball with Zach and some boys we met while playing over the Spring. They weren't what you would consider prospects, but what was I to do? It was all I had to work with at the time, and I needed to practice bad. The pro players practiced every day I supposed, so naturally I would do the same, well, when Grammy didn't need me doing my chores anyhow.

There were always things to do around the house and because it was just the two of us now, things fell on me more than they once had. I was sure about one thing, though. Eric Davis was practicing, and so I just got my mindset into that same groove. If he was practicing, I would be practicing. Besides, we loved to play ball. The warmer weather was nice, and the field, although more dirt than grass, was always free of people for some reason. We felt like it was our field, and we had called it McFarland Field since those days I spent chasing after Davey and his friends to play there. No one else called it that, to be fair. Honestly, no one else called it anything other than "The Ball Field." So, McFarland Field just felt right and had a good ring to it. Besides, Davey came up with the name, and he was playing for college now, so anyone that wanted a different name had better be a Minor Leaguer or better, because Davey had that up on everyone else around town.

Zach was a decent pitcher, and although he did not throw very hard, he was accurate. This made for a decent practice outing for me. He could almost always get it straight over the plate and so the need for a catcher was nonexistent for the most part. I could just hit flyball after flyball without having to stop every time he threw one just a little outside or was thrown for a ball. The field did not have a backstop, so we sometimes made our own out of old trashcans from the entranceway to the park. If they were filled, we would have to drag them over. If they smelled God awful, we just played without them there to stop wild throws. I would much rather stop and retrieve the ball, than to smell a pile of rotting garbage someone had tossed away God knows when.

One day we were all there and some older kids came and rode their bikes all over the field, kicking up dust and grabbing the ball whenever we hit it out past the pitcher. We had only 3 baseballs so each time they took one and threw it around the field at one and other, we had to hope they would not get another from us. I tried to hit it away from them, but they would just ride quickly over to where an outfielder was and threaten to smash him if they did not give him the ball.

We went home with no baseballs that day, and practice was over quickly. It was discouraging but I would just find more baseballs somewhere, I reasoned. Zach had tennis balls at his house that his brother found at a yard sale, and so we would hit those when we had no more baseballs left to lose. They were much easier to hit, but the feeling of the bat rattling off your hands if you did not grip it just tight enough when the hard baseball connected with it, was gone. I liked the tennis balls also because if Zach threw a little inside, I was not ducking for cover. Only once did he pluck me on the head, and that was when I was most thankful for his lack of speed and power behind those pitches of his.

Davey was calling at 6 PM one evening, and so I hurried home to make sure I did not miss his call.

"Hey, squirt, how are things with Grammy going? What's going on with you?" he said when he first heard my voice.

Squirt was a lot nicer than most things he called me years ago, so I was good with it. Besides, Davey and I got along much better as we got older, and that made me smile. I always liked Davey. Wanting to be more like him was a constant thought. He was stronger, older, and liked by everyone. Plus, when he was a star in high school, he let me tag along occasionally when he'd go to McFarland Field for a pickup game. I was always taking the position of backstop, but I truly did not mind. Watching my big brother rip hits forcefully all over that field was awesome. He could hit the ball clear over the fence and into the brush, but then most times it was impossible to find the ball until winter came and the overgrown weeds and wild fruit bushes died off. Then, kids would be roaming the weeds looking for any souvenir balls they could find. Davey did not mind. After all, the school allowed him, or at least that is the story he told us, to take balls home to practice his Ruthian swing, he called it.

"Hey! Hey, Davey!" I replied excitedly. "Have you gotten any more playing time? What's it like playing on a college team? Have you hit any home runs yet? Are any scouts checking you out yet, Davey? Are they?"

"Slow down, Squirt. Listen. They told me this upcoming season to expect more playing time. A few of the older guys graduated and so they need more guys to step up and fill their spots on the roster. I'm trying hard, Ronnie. It's a lot different from high school ball at Red Creek, that's for sure. The pitchers throw harder and have insane control of where they pitch. The other guys are strong hitters, and I am always trying to catch them. It reminds me of you playing ball when we were kids, and always trying to catch up so you could go the field with us older kids. It's a lot like that. But don't you worry. As soon as I know I am starting a game, I will let you and Grammy know, and you both can come and watch me play. I won't forget to tell you, okay?"

Davey talked a little while longer, and then he wanted to talk with Grammy. He only had so much time because he had to get back to his studies. Davey was always smart, but this was more intense than he had expected, and with the extra added pressure of having to work twice as hard at his strength and conditioning daily, it was just a lot on him. Grammy did not understand that all. She was always trying to tell Davey to slow down. To smell the roses more. To look at the dandelions on the field and remember that everything and everyone had a purpose, no matter what he or she thought about it. It all had purpose and it all mattered. Otherwise, it was senseless to grow or live at all. That was what she learned from Grandad. Each and every little thing had a distinct purpose on this planet, even if we did not know what that purpose was. It simply did not matter what we thought.

I heard Grammy tell Davey about Momma. He must have asked how she was doing, and Grammy usually always said the same thing.

"She's doing okay, David, not great but the doctors say she is coming along. I know it's a lot to think about, but trust Grammy. I am always talking to the doctors and sending her letters so that the nurses can read them to her. You have a lot on your plate, David. Worry about that. This is exactly what your momma wanted for you and let me tell you this. She will be proud as a peacock when she gets out and sees all you have done."

I stopped believing Grammy about Momma getting out long ago. It just seemed like she was telling us whatever we wanted to hear to satisfy our desires to have her with us again, instead of what was really going on. The last time I saw Momma was several months ago, and her hair was thinning, her clothes laid loosely on her declining frame.

She looked as if her skin was a pale shade, and her high cheekbones were sharper against her face. She did not walk much at all, and although I always talked to her and told her all about what had been going on back at home, I am not sure she even knew who I was, or what I was talking about. She would sometimes smile, but it was more random and with no true purpose behind it. I hated going there to visit her, but it was the only way I was able to even talk to her. Calling her did no good. She had stopped talking long ago. I had forgotten what she sounded like almost entirely, and that part hurt the most.

I swore one day I would get her out of there and back home where she belonged. Maybe she would find her voice again if she were around her family all the time. Maybe seeing her familiar house, and her old wood furniture, and that front porch swing we always rocked in would jog her memory. Grammy said she wished that were possible, and that one day it would be, but that today was not that day. I hated it, but Grammy was just trying to let me down easy, while still giving me some hope to hang on to. She was good at that. Giving me hope.

When Grammy hung up the phone with Davey, she asked if I wanted to go see Momma in a few weeks. She could wait until Davey had a few days to take a breather from his studies and his playing, and we could all head over together and make a small trip of it. I thought that sounded perfect but wished that Janet and Thelma Louise could go as well. Janet was simply too far and for her to come back at the same time Davey was able to was nearly impossible. Thelma

Louise had her hands full with her two kids, plus her husband who sometimes felt like a third child, Grammy said. Besides, she did not like to see Momma. Not like that anyhow. It pained her to see her shuffling back and forth, incoherent, and out of sorts. Thelma Louise just wanted Momma out of that "Wacky Insane Hospital," as she called it, and home where she belonged.

When I knew we were going to see Momma, I would head to my room and open my brown shoebox. Moving the mound of baseball cards I had collected over the years, I would dig down and pull out my green spiral book I had been given by Janet years back. In it, I still wrote notes about things I wanted to and needed to know, when I was older. The questions were still gathering on the pages, and I had no intentions of stopping that. It was important for me to ensure I remembered all the questions I had so they all got answers at some point. Questions always needed answers, I figured. It made total sense to me. Why would anyone ask a question that didn't have an answer? Even if one did not know the answer, one could always find the answer. So, I made sure that notebook was safe where it had been for years now.

When the day came, Davey pulled in and unloaded some of his dirty clothes. He figured he could save some time by doing his laundry at Grammy's house while staying away from school for a few days. Grammy just told him to put it on the floor inside and she would tend to it later when they got back. He need not worry about that. He gave Grammy a big hug, and she smiled at him, holding him tight, and telling him how happy she was to see him. Davey, she knew, would have a hard time when we got to where Momma was, so she always tried to give him a little extra loving before we left. Davey saw me standing behind Grammy and grabbed my head, rubbing his knuckles back and forth over the top, and said,

"Hey, Squirt. You been good for Grammy? You aren't giving her any trouble, are ya? I don't want to have to come back from school and fix it for you."

Grammy would tell him to hush it. She told him I was never any trouble, and I was the easiest one out of all of the grandkids that she helped raise. She smiled half-jokingly when she said it, but she probably meant it anyway. I was easy. Never did I backtalk Grammy. Besides, if I did, she could backhand me and knock sense into me. She may be old, but she was still a tough broad. That's what my friend's parents would say. They would ask me how the tough old broad was doing. It wasn't meant to be mean. They just knew all that Grammy had gone through and the difficult hand she had been dealt with Momma's issues and Grandad's passing. They knew she had taken a second life on when she agreed to raise us. No way was she letting us go to a home. Having one child in a sort of home was bad enough. Her grandkids were not heading to another one, not over her dead body.

As we headed out, Davey sat in the front seat. I was sitting in the back and I was reminded of the time we all drove out to see Momma for the first time. I remembered being nervous but excited. As I glared silently out the window, I saw so many colored license plates and I was brought back to a different time. One where my sister Janet told me to see how many I could find. Now I realized the purpose of that. She wanted to keep my mind off things bothering me, and that was why she had come up with that game. She did not care how many different license plates we saw on the way there and how many more or less we saw on the way back. She just wanted to relax me and take my mind off what I was about to see. Janet was like that, always thinking two steps ahead. Knowing what was coming and how to get around it before it came was her specialty. Maybe that is the reason she went to school for engineering. She could solve just about any problem thrown at her, so it was more like engineering picked her, over her picking it.

Davey didn't pay any attention back then to Janet and her license plate game, he just sat straight with his ears opened and straining, trying to hear the conversation that Grammy and Thelma Louise were having. I remembered that trip well, almost as if it were just yesterday, but I realized it was several years ago now, and we were all in different places in our lives.

The ride did not seem as long as it once had, and the roads were a little less filled with construction. I also did not have to pee, so that made it seem a lot less far away. When we passed the spot where Grammy had pulled off to let me pee, that field where I had taken a few steps into so no one could see what it was I was doing, I noticed there was a sign on the road that explained what was going on there. Four new office buildings were being planned, and they were renting out space in advance. I was taken aback at first, the speed at which that land was being changed over, but I quickly realized it was not all that fast. It had sat as open land since the beginning of time, and now it was going to actually be something else. All the weeds and brush and rocks and trees would be cleared out to make room for office buildings where hundreds of people would begin their careers or continue them in a new setting.

It was strange only for a minute, until I thought back to Grandad and our drives. How he pointed to so many unimportant places and explained how it was so much different when he was a kid running around. Now, it was me that got to see change, and places being constructed where I had once simply pulled over to pee in a field. I wondered if anyone cared that hundreds, if not thousands of people had pulled over onto that same broken gravel shoulder, walked into the high rough brush, pulled down their fly, and just peed all over. Probably not, I supposed. When you got to go, you got to go. Besides, soon, no one would be peeing outside. From now on, they could just walk into those shiny glass front doors, walk over to the bathroom, open the door to the urinal, and pee like adults. Things were changing for sure.

When we approached the gate this time, things were also very different than they were on the first trip we made. The guard was a different man and a little nicer than the original one. He smiled when we pulled up, recognizing Grammy from our last visit, and just waved her in, without the need to stop. The old metal rusted gate was also no longer standing. They had replaced it with an automated gate that opened when you got close enough to it. Sensors were built in to detect a car coming, and slowly but steadily, it would open, and we would simply drive on through. The parking lot was in the same area, but you no longer had to wait for someone to come out and direct you in. You just walked over to the entrance, and they buzzed you in. Then you went to the front reception area and they put your name on a badge you had to display on your person and walked to the elevator to head to your floor. When you arrived at your chosen floor, you walked out and over to another set of doors and rang the buzzer. This time the voice would click back and say, "can I help you?" and you would tell them who you were there to see. In this instance, it was "We are here to see Dolores McFarland, please." The doors would be opened from a desk further away, and you would walk into the reception area there. Then, they would greet you and tell you to wait a moment while they prepared Momma for us. I assumed that meant ensuring she was decent, well, as decent as she could be under the circumstances. We would walk behind a nurse over to where Momma's room was, and the nurse would turn and say,

"If you all need anything, just yell for one of us and we will come and take care of you."

It was so different, a better place overall from what I remembered from all those years back, but it was still not home. And it was still my momma in here. So, they could have painted the walls rainbow with polka dots. It would not make it nice. Thankfully though, it was a lot cleaner. Another company had apparently purchased it from the previous owners, and had money to clean things up, and to make the rooms nicer and hire better people. What a change just a few years had made, I thought to myself. All of this had been changed a little at a time, each time we were back home, and Momma was here. She had seen all the changes, but I am not sure she knew that it had taken place. Seeing something, and actually understanding it, were two entirely different things.

Davey shuffled over to Momma first and pushed his lips to the top of her head. He held them there a moment and then cleared his throat before saying,

"Hi, Momma. It's nice to see you."

Momma did not look up. She just looked out into nothing, but she managed a smile. We never knew if the smiles were for us, or for a thought she had in her head that had entered at that same moment, making it just a coincidence. I guess it did not matter much, because at least she had smiled. Davey could believe she saw him or heard him, and that that smile was for him. Even if it wasn't true. The truth is no one knew. Not me, not Grammy, not Davey, and not the nurses, despite what they thought they knew. No, maybe Momma knew. Maybe she was the only one who knew what was going on in her head.

I like to think when she heard our voices, that she was taken back to a time long ago when we were young. A time when she could gently swing with us or have an ice cream cone on a hot sticky summer's day. Or maybe even further back, to when she was a little girl and Grandad and Grammy would walk with her side by side, holding her each with one of their hands as they simultaneously swung her back and forth off the ground and laughed. Grandad told me once that no matter whatever happened in life, the past was always the past. Our memories were always what they were, and although we may forget some things, the true moments in life we treasured, we could never truly forget. The small things would become the big moments for us as we got older. He liked the small things. Running in the theatre to get out of the rain with Grammy. Having an ice cream cone with me for no reason at all. Changing a tire for some poor guy who had blown one out and did not have the know-how to fix it himself.

Those were the moments Grandad said would be most important when our time came. Not the big things like the job we had, or the overtime we took one week to pay for a new shingled roof. Not even your actual wedding day. That day was a big day for sure, but it was the next day that truly mattered, when you sat across from your new blushing bride, and it sunk in that you were now a husband. Everyone had a happy wedding day, he said. The next day was much more important. The way you treated that second day was what mattered most. There was importance in the quiet moment when you realized that all the excitement from the night before was over, and you understood you were living with your new reality. Looking at the woman across from you, now your wife, having a drink on the porch, or folding clothes, or getting up to head to bed and loving those small moments. Those were the times he would miss most, he told me. I imagined he did, because Grammy still did those things, and he was just not there to see them anymore.

I looked at Grammy, and she nodded and motioned her hands towards Momma as if to tell me to go over and say hi. So, I did. I walked over and looked at Davey for a second, who just tried to keep a positive look on his face for me, but inside I knew he was hurting for her.

"Momma? It's me, Ronnie. Hi Momma. I'm glad to see you. Guess what? I am trying out for the baseball team at school. I've been practicing every day and I really think I have a good chance this year. Maybe you will be able to come to one of my games soon and you will see me in my uniform. I know it's not a tie and suit, but it's close, Momma. They are Red and Ivory, just like the real Cincinnati Reds. One day Momma, one day, you will be at a game where Davey and I are both playing, and you can cheer from the stands and tell everyone that both of your boys are in the game. One day Momma."

We talked to her for about an hour as if she were home with us, and sometimes talking to each other while she just sat and stared at different things along the floor or out in the hall. A nurse came in on two different occasions to give her meds and to take her blood pressure, but for the most part, we were alone with her. Grammy shared with Momma all that she was doing with the house, how the neighbors across the way lost all their chickens to a sly fox because some idiot had left the gate open to the pen, and how both

Janet and Thelma Louise wish they could have been able to see her today but could not. She told her about Janet's grades and how she had a perfect 4.0 grade point average once again, and how soon she would land a big fancy job just like Momma had wanted for her and always envisioned.

That made Grammy proud. Proud for two reasons. First, because Momma had wanted this so bad for us before she got sick, and second, because Grammy herself had played a big role in raising us while Momma could not and helped us all get to where we were. She never bragged about it. Never asked for thanks for any of it, but she was proud of herself for being such an instrumental person in our lives. We all knew it, though, and we were grateful for her and all she did. Still, it was time we had more of Momma. That was not getting easier on any of us, and Grammy was getting older and noticeably slower, and it was becoming more apparent that time was not going to slow down. I had no idea of what any of us could do to fix any of that.

Chapter 15

The Brother of a Star

* * *

When you attended high school in Red Creek, Pennsylvania, you did one of three things; You played sports, you watched others play sports, or you did neither, but you had to hear about it just the same. Everyone in town always liked to talk about what their team did the night before, or how this would be the year they went to states and finally beat their rivals, bringing home the trophy, but more important, the bragging rights for a full year.

Red Creek had never had a championship, and although my brother Davey was such a standout player, the rest of the team had been subpar, and he could not carry them through the playoffs on his own. We had not won a single playoff game since as long as I could remember. The folks in town talked about teams in the 70s that had produced great results, but even those teams had never been able to bring home bragging rights. This included football as well, which Davey never played. Oh, he wanted to play both sports, but coach Hickson talked Davey out of that after his freshman year at Red Creek High. Davey had a scare in the second game of the season, when he was returning a kickoff and was hit hard enough to flatten him out like an oak plank board, and it took several minutes for Davey to come to. Grammy was just as happy, though. She did not enjoy seeing her grandson laid flat out, helpless, as he had been. Davey did not complain much and put up a minimal fight at best. To him, he just wanted to do whatever he was best at, and after that hit, he realized he was not best at taking big hits he did not see coming.

Zach and I went out for the team together. We brought our old, weathered mitts with us, and although I did not own a pair of my own cleats, Davey had left a pair behind and Grammy said it would be perfectly fine for me to wear those. They were a little big, so we added newspaper in the toes, so they did not fall off when I ran. I tied them extra tight as well, and they weren't all that bad after that.

When we got to the field, my stomach knotted up quickly. There were so many other Red Creek boys, and a few girls as well, throwing to one another, hitting in the metal batting cages, and talking about what they did the night before and laughing all about it. Honestly, this was not what I had expected, and I really just wanted to head home. Zach, though, made me stay. He knew how important this was to me, and besides, we had just as much right to be here as anyone else. Maybe even more so, because we had practiced on our own all year, without the luxury of a coach to guide us in the right direction. Some of these kids had played travel summer ball, where they would meet other teams from around the state and play exhibitions. A few times they even went into Ohio and played ball with kids from that state as well.

"McFarland, get over here," shouted the coach as soon as he saw me. Ugh, talk about pressure. He knew my name, probably because of my brother Davey, and now in front of all these other kids, he was basically singling me out. No pressure, just breath in and out. In and out, I kept telling myself. Zach told me I better hurry, because making the coach wait was a bad first move.

"Yes, coach?"

"So, you are David's kid brother, huh. You any good? You going to be the next David McFarland for our team, son?" he said in a manner that felt like he was condescending in some way, but hopeful in another.

I was feeling a giant lump in my throat, and quickly I could feel the eyes of dozens of kids looking at the coach and me talking, and knew they realized who I was and were probably curious. You could not miss the era of Davey McFarland if you tried. He had broken school records for hits, stolen bases, and was just 13 home runs shy of that record as well. Second best was not too bad, especially when your high school had been around for decades. He had a banner on the field with his name on it, and the trophy case that lacked a state championship, did not lack Davey's name. It seemed as if every other trophy was a David McFarland showpiece.

Now here I was, the kid brother. Trying to just make

the team, and I had not even been on the field for 15 minutes and I had a target on my back already. The other kids were commenting in the not too distant background, saying things like,

"Hey, David's brother. Going to show your brother up and steal those records of his?"

"Oh, look, it's McFarland 2.0. He's come to save us all and finally bring that state title to Red Creek."

They were snickering and taunting, and then the coach told me to pay them no mind.

"Listen son, don't bother listening to them. This is not about your brother, it's about you. If you can hang, you can make your own name for yourself. Just give me what you have, and I'll do the rest. Deal?"

As I walked back over to where Zach was standing alone, looking around as if he had no idea what to do, I could feel everyone's eyes on me, hot and intense, like the first morning sun in August. I could feel them staring at me with wonder and judgement, and I just wanted to get back to Zach and not worry about any of it anymore.

Being the brother of a star high school player had its perks, but little did I know or understand that it also came with disadvantages. I had big shoes to fill and was trying to fill them now. I felt as if the shoes I had stuffed that old newspaper into to fit properly, were now loosening. Maybe it was that the paper was breaking down from walking in them, or maybe it was just my mind playing a trick on me. I wished Davey were there with me, though. He would know what to tell me. He would know just what to do in the situation at hand. Plus, no one would be snickering and commenting from all sides of the field if he were there. They would be in awe of him, knowing they had only seen him play as younger kids. Knowing their parents would come home from the games talking about how that great David McFarland kid was going places. How he had a great game and boy, you should have seen that inside the park home run hit in the third inning, causing the other team to be drained of any momentum they had brought with them to the game.

Davey was a legend in Red Creek, and he would know just how to help me. We did not get to practice much anymore because he was always away at school and practicing there and studying to ensure his scholarship stayed intact. Most important was that scholarship. He would need to maintain a certain grade point average or risk losing it. He struggled at first with his classes, but after his school hired a tutor to get him on track, Davey managed to do just that. He got back on track and swore he would stay there. An education and degree were important to him, more than playing pro ball. Davey knew that the chances of ever playing in the Minors, let alone the Major League level, were slim to none. I had faith, though. I felt Davey could do just about damn near anything he put his mind to. Grammy did as well.

Out west, Janet was in her final year of her four-year degree and had decided to pursue a master's degree right after. She loved going to school, and learning was something she excelled at. Her grade point average never dropped, and she got some grants and scholarship money that freed her up just enough to give her some much-needed repose. Her time away from home was hard on everyone, but it was exactly what she needed. To get out of that old dusty town and find herself. She was always trying to figure out what she would do with her life in Red Creek, and now she did not have to. The world was knocking at her door and opportunity was looming all around her.

Grammy always told Janet that a fish only grows as large as the bowl would allow it to. If she stayed in Red Creek, she could only grow as big as Red Creek would let her, but if she moved on from this small town, to a bigger place, a different place, she could grow as large as her world allowed. Janet did not want to be in a small fishbowl, because she had big dreams and plans. She intended to grow on the outside while away at school, and then maybe come back east and find work somewhere near home, but that thought changed after her first semester.

Janet loved the area and people of Washington. The diversity she had not had the chance to be around in Red Creek was intriguing to her. All the different cultures and people and thought patterns they came with fascinated her. She enjoyed learning about where they had come from, and what their family backgrounds were like. Coming from the town we had, we knew only what we could see with our own eyes. There was an enormous world out there, and she quickly learned that even though her life was not an easy journey at all, she had friends who had escaped so much more than she could ever imagine. Some of her friends had come from as far away as China, and some were local to the school. Each had a story of their own to share, and each felt the others were strong for coming as far as they had.

Janet found deep appreciation for the landscape her new home offered and the way the weather cast different shadows over the seasons than she was accustomed to. She enjoyed hiking in the summer months when school was closed and sitting under the twinkling bright stars at night wondering what dreams she should be pursuing next. She thought of Grammy and me back home, and how we were getting along with things and how wonderful it would be to share her new surroundings with us.

She talked with Davey at least once a month, but she could tell he was struggling a little with school and so she tried to send encouraging words his way. When she thought of Thelma Louise, she smiled, thinking about the mother she was becoming, and she was sad when she felt that Thelma Louise had missed her chance at school and eventually reaching all of her potential. But mostly, she thought about Momma. How she was in that building with no family close by, and how she had not been able to travel out and see her in some time. It bothered her, being all the way out in Washington, while Momma was all the way here, alone, in Ohio. When she called me, she always asked when Grammy and I were going out to visit Momma and made me promise to kiss her on her head and to tell her that that particular kiss was from Janet. She said she would be out to visit just as soon as she could get back east, but even in the summer months, she had to work almost daily to keep up with her expenses and her studies.

So, life went on, and we all settled into our routines as best we could. We were each in different places, and different times in our journeys, but we were all family still. We had gone through so much together and had stuck it out in a way that most people may have thought quite impossible, all things considered. We owed that to the people raising us.

Grandad had been such a powerful and positive influence in our lives that we had to be grateful for the time we had with him here. While we were sad he was gone, he still seemed to guide us with his invaluable advice, and his ability to see the good in just about damn near anything. Even weeds.

Grammy had taken over for Momma when she first suffered her sickness, and although she was done raising children of her own, she quickly settled into that role once again when she was most needed. She did not have to do that, and I am not sure anyone would have blamed her had she not. Four kids alone, without their mother and fathers around. Without the help of her best friend and husband by her side, pitching in where he could. Without much of anything at all. Grammy had never complained, at least not that I ever heard from her, about the cards she was dealt. She simply played the hand.

I know she hated that Momma was where she was, but she always said there was a plan for all of us, even if we did not quite understand it. We would someday. She said this when I would ask why Grandad had to die when he did. She knew there was a plan for him and why he had to leave her, even though she did not understand it at all. It hurt her, but she would still smile and talk about all the times she had spent by his side, instead of the times she had not. The time she did had was more important to her than the time she did not. If she focused on the time she'd lost, she felt she was casting an ungrateful shadow on the time she'd been gifted with Grandad.

Momma. We owed her a great deal. More than anything. Here was a woman who had seen her first husband die tragically. She remarried and had that man turn out to be anything but a decent man. On top of that, there was my father, whoever that may be, not around to help raise me. I stopped inquiring about my father because Grammy told me when the time was right, she would let me know more. I wrote it in my notebook because that was one of the questions I would have answered for certain. It I had just never been the right time, I guess. Momma had also lost her father, whom she simply adored. Grandad and she were tight. Real tight. She always respected him, and he always tried to give her a little more than he probably should, because he wanted her happy. Although he did not agree with all her life decisions, he rarely told her that. If she asked for advice, he was all too pleased to give that to her. If she did not, he did not want to get in her way. It was her life, and her journey to complete. Who was he to change the course of all of that?

We had great people surrounding us and to complain about what we could not change was senseless. The world was big, and opportunities were plentiful. We just had to take the right steps and choose the right paths. It was most important to take steps in the right direction, no matter how big or how small those steps were. If we had dreams and goals, we would do what we could to make them our reality. I know Thelma Louise had dreams. She had goals. But those changed when she met Mike and had her two beautiful children and she accepted that sometimes we must adjust our goals and what we want out of life. Davey seemed to do that as well. Although he had dreamed of being a ballplayer since the days we were young kids, he knew that at some point he would need to create a different set of goals for himself. If being a ballplayer did not pan out the way he hoped, he would be something else. Something that suited him even better than playing ball, something he felt was a calling.

When the first practice of the season was over, I felt defeated. I had done extraordinarily little to show I was a ballplayer, and even less to show I was the younger brother of Davey McFarland. Zach told me it was only the first practice and to be patient, but I just felt so down about it all. It had not gone according to plan. The ball was much faster coming at me than I had imagined. The kids were faster, too. So fast. I was shocked at how some of the girls were outrunning some of the boys. The kids were bigger as well. I was growing more, but these kids just felt head and shoulders above me and Zach. I felt like a runt on the field compared to them, and to top it off, I had dropped three easy flyballs in the outfield, and that was so unlike me.

Something was off, and I had to hope it was just first

day jitters. From the start, I felt uneasy about the prospect of walking onto the field with all the expectations of being Davey McFarland's little brother, heavy on my back. By the end of that first practice, the only thing that would let anyone know I was Davey's brother was my last name.

When I got back to Grammy's, I threw my glove on the front porch, took off the cleats that did not fit anyway, and tossed them in a box by the front door. Grammy saw me come in and was cooking something in the kitchen. She did not even look my way but asked me how things had gone, as she continued to focus on whatever it was she was making.

"Jasper, tough day?" she asked.

I did not want to talk about it just yet, so I silently walked in, opened the refrigerator to grab the lemonade out, then grabbed a tall glass and poured me a cup. Taking a long sip, I sat down at the kitchen counter and just put my head down on the table below.

"Grammy, why do I always feel as if I am chasing things? Nothing seems to come easy, and well, I thought this was going to be different for once. Why is it that even baseball is running from me?"

"Well, if you want something easy, what does that say about you and who you truly are? You are trying to tell me you don't want that immense feeling of excitement from working for it? That the easy road is the one you want to travel because it is the simpler path? Jasper, now how fun would that be? Think about it this way. Whatever that ballplayer's name is you like, do you think he just walked onto the field one day and hit all those home runs, just as if he were born that way? No. He had to work hard for it. Day after day. Week after week. Year after year. I bet nothing was easy for him, but you know what? He did it, and he can now look back at all the hard work and struggling that happened along the way and know that it shaped him to who he is today. Without that, I promise you, he would not be the player you watch on the TV. No sir, not even close. He earned that."

Why did she always need to make such good sense of things? I just wanted to sulk and drown myself in the cold lemonade I had in front of me, but she had a way of helping me see things from a different viewpoint every time. I loved Grammy for that, as much as I hated that she was always right. She was always able to see the good in things and the positive in even the bad moments. She didn't take credit for that though. She told me that it was Grandad's doing. That he had taught her to view things with a different, more positive perspective. Even the smallest of things. Anytime he saw something that others saw as insignificant, he knew those people were closed minded and lacked appreciation for possibilities. It was not what we saw, that mattered. It was what was actually beyond what we saw. He had an ability to see past what was right in front of him, straight to the importance and potential in even the most seemingly inconsequential of things.

Imagine seeing a humble weed, a bright yellow dandelion growing straight up out of a small insignificant crack in the sidewalk, reaching with such desire for the sun. Proud and firm and unaware that it is a weed to begin with. How did the seed first get there? Most folks would never think about it from that perspective, he said. It did not matter, though, because the seed had arrived there somehow, whether it belonged there or not. Maybe it blew from the front yard the past fall and had waited all winter for its moment to shine, or maybe a lazy bird had dropped it from high above, just so, and it landed perfectly beneath the imperfect concrete walk. The Spring rain had given it a drink to quench its thirst, and the morning sun hit it just right. All those steps were needed for that green weed to mature, and peak out with its brilliant yellow flower, and grow. No one had come by to pick it out of the crack, and so it was allowed to flourish, untouched. That weed stood as a reminder that we need to allow ourselves to flourish, he'd remind me over and over, until it was our time to be picked from where we had sprouted. Then, we passed that lesson and life on down to someone else. We set the example of how to grow in the most unassuming places and circumstances, and thrive, nonetheless, showing others that it was indeed possible. The surroundings for which we were forced to grow need not be ideal. It was what we were built of and the ingredients we channeled inside ourselves, that mattered most. That is what allowed those dandelions to sing as they did on those warm summer mornings. Everything has purpose, and everything, a meaning beyond what we are even meant to understand. That's just the way it is. Purpose is not what we want it to be. It's simply what is meant to be.

Chapter 16

That Little Girl

* * *

Purpose. The word itself had never meant all that much to me, but somehow, I was always drawn back to it. What was my exact purpose here, and would I truly be able to see it once it showed itself? Would my purpose be to play professional ball and help a team and city feel pride by bringing home victories, or was my purpose something on a much smaller scale, but still maybe just as important to someone in need? Not knowing what purpose actually meant, I was sorely confused. This was a question I knew Grandad could have answered, but he was not around any longer to do so. I asked Grammy if she would mind driving me over to where Grandad was buried, so I could talk with him some. She told me I could always talk to Grandad no matter where I was at, but that she thought it was a wonderful idea to go over and sit with him for a while.

"Jasper, would you mind if I sat beside you when you are with Grandad? It's been a little while for me as well, and I would love to feel like the three of us are once again enjoying the warm gentle sun together, like we used to do. Would that be okay?"

It was always okay in my mind. Grammy was like my best friend, even better than Zach was. She just understood me from the start. She was kind but firm, and I liked her balance on that. Maybe she was trying to make up for something in her past, or maybe she just loved the way she made her grandchildren feel like they were her very own children. Had we not had our Momma, she would have been my next pick for one. She was very kind, and caring, and quick as a whip with her responses. Maybe she had a lot of Grandad in her too because he was exactly the same.

That next morning, we jumped in her truck, the one that was Grandad's back when he was still alive, and began our trip over to visit with him. We did not pack a picnic this time, though. This was a different type of morning and we really just wanted to enjoy the early sun on our faces, while we sat and talked. Nothing fancy, just her and me and Grandad.

When we arrived, it seemed other folks had the same idea for that particular day. There were people walking over to stones and laying flowers down or holding one another closely as they just stared at the hard ground beneath their feet. I watched for a few moments, wondering who they had lost that meant so much to them. I'm certain there were many stones that had not seen visitors for many years, and that was a sad thought in my mind. But these people had folks visiting them and leaving flowers or hand-drawn notes. Some shedding tears and some casting pleasant smiles in their directions.

I saw a woman sitting Indian style, picking the blades of grass from the ground in front of her with no rhyme or reason, just talking. I could not hear the words she was speaking in that instance, but she was sad. Her words were directed to a small, curved stone that stood no more than a foot high and was a pale pink color. Grammy looked over at me as I watched this young woman sit there, grabbing a blade at a time from the ground and tossing it gently towards the stone. She stayed for a little and then, she put back on her shoes, stood up, and walked away, with her head still down towards the ground, back to her car and drove away. As we opened the doors to our truck, I asked Grammy if it would be all right if I walked by that stone to see who that young woman was visiting, and she thought it would be all right to do so.

When I arrived at the stone, I looked around to see if anyone was watching me and noticed that everyone else in the cemetery was focused on what they were there to do, and nothing else. So, I knelt where that woman had just been and looked at the stone. There was a name, and a birth date, and a death date inscribed on the stone, and it read:

Anna Marie Pyle
Beloved daughter
Born August 21, 1996
Died August 23, 1996

She had been only two days old and had passed just about a year ago. Here I was, standing over top of this tiny little girl, who had only lived for two days, but she had clearly made an impact in the two short days she had on this earth. Her mother, I assumed anyway it was her mother, had come to visit with her child as I do with Grandad, and to talk with her. Why? Because she had a purpose in those two days she was here. That time was just long enough to make a lasting impression on people and then it was simply her time to go. I never understood what made it time to go, and who and why that was all decided, but it was so. She could not control her time, only what she did with the time she had been given. Time was a gift, and she had two days to leave her gift here before she moved on. I wanted to remember this little girl, and this particular moment. I reached into my pocket, pulled out my notebook and a pencil, worn down to the eraser almost by now, and wrote a note to myself:

"Anna Marie Pyle, dies after just 2 days on this earth. What was her purpose in being here in the first place, if she was just going to leave right away and cause pain for someone left behind?"

After that, I put my spiral notebook back in my back pocket. By this time, it was bending and curled at the corners and they were peeling off, showing the brown cardboard beneath the once sharp green edges. Pages had been pulled out and slid back in so they would not be lost, but I could not bring myself to start another one. This notebook had a special meaning. It had a purpose, and that I knew and understood well.

By the time I got back to Grammy, she had settled in

and was sitting alongside Grandad's stone, and she was smiling at me, straining somewhat with the bright sun in her face. I could see her age in that light, and it made me understand that time was not slowing down for her at all.

"Did you get the answer to your question while over there, Jasper?"

"Well, Grammy, I did, and I didn't. Some of it made sense, but other parts did not."

She just chuckled some and told me that life was like that. Some things made complete and total sense, while other things made about as much sense as a giant whale desiring to eat tiny plankton in the ocean with all the other large things they had around them. Why God had made such a humongous creature that ate one of the smallest living things on earth, was beyond her comprehension. But that is what made life interesting, she thought. After all, if everything made complete sense to us, and it all was so easily understood, what fun would life be? We would always know what to expect, when to expect it, and just how to respond to it all. It would not allow for creative thinking or require problem-solving skills. Think of Janet out in Washington state. Imagine if she did not need to work on ideas, complex math, and concepts to figure out solutions to intricate affairs. What would be her purpose then? And there was that word again. Purpose. Everything on this planet had it, even if we did not understand the why of it.

"Grammy, is it alright if I talk to Grandad in my mind, or do you think he needs to hear it out loud?"

"No, I think in your mind, as long as it is from your heart, is just how he would want to hear it. You do that talking how you like, Jasper, but be sure you pull it from your heart. That will be when the words have the right meaning, and you will learn the true answers you need," she said.

So, I sat alongside Grammy, and looked out over the wide field of different colored stones, with the sun hitting the quartz buried within those pretty monuments and bouncing around like diamonds against a dark backdrop. Each of these stones had a reminder of someone that had once walked where I walk and looked out at the very moon I see in the evening. Each person laying now below the surface had been something to someone and if they were now forgotten, that made me sad. Time took away what it had once created, and that was hard for me to swallow. One day I may not be a memory at all, and my stone will go unattended, unvisited, by anyone, ever again. Just a name and two dates chiseled deep into its polished surface. Maybe for a generation or two it would be graced by visitors, but then what? Why would they need my monument glistening in the sun like raindrops if I would just be forgotten eventually, anyway?

Looking back at where Grandad was now, I built a hope he would always have his visitors. He needed people to stop by and say a simple hello to him because he genuinely loved people. All kinds, he did. People fascinated him because they always did things in ways he would not have. Some he thought were downright crazy and some he felt were bordering brilliant. Both, he respected, though. Without both, he said, we would not understand what a true genius thought was, after all. It would all just be normal, basic, boring thinking, and what fun would that be?

In my mind, I talked to Grandad, and I was making sure it came from deep in my heart, as Grammy had told me to do. I told him that after all this time, I still missed our little talks, and the times we would go to the trails for long walks, or fishing, or even just for ice cream in town. I told him how deeply I missed having Momma home with us in the kitchen, sitting at the counter with her fresh morning coffee as if all was right with the world.

The simplest things I missed. I could do without baseball, without making it big one day. I did not want to do things without knowing Momma was ok, and I begged him to talk with God about that for me. To help Momma get well enough, that we could bring her back home with us, back to where she belonged. It was time, I felt. She had been away almost as long as he had and losing two of the three most important people in our lives hurt deep down, and it made no sense at all. I could maybe understand losing one person, as hard as that was. After all, we all lose people that mean a great deal to us, but losing two of the most important people, well, that was just plain wrong in my opinion. It felt greedy to take two. Then I talked to him about Grammy. I told him he would be so proud of all she had done for us while he was gone. That she had helped both Davey and Janet get to college so they could prove to the world they belonged doing greater things than Red

Creek would allow. I told him she was proud of Thelma Louise for the mother she had become, even if her husband Mike was a sorry SOB.

Now, I was the final one left, and I was scared. Scared for what was to come. Having no pre-determined plan, or set goals to chase after, other than to be a Major Leaguer, which honestly felt like it was too far from even a possibility now, was difficult. How would I know what I was supposed to be doing, and when should I start on that? What, exactly was my purpose here? I asked him to please help me see my purpose in it all. I was afraid to fail and disappoint both Grammy and Momma. Anything but that.

When I finished talking to him, I looked over at Grammy, and noticed she must have been doing the exact same thing I was. Only this time around, when we were just about to depart, she did not have that same look of wanting to cry. She smiled as if she were totally okay with how things were today. Placing her arm around my shoulders, she pulled me in close to her, and whispered into my ear,

"Jasper, I am so proud of you. You make Grammy very happy, and that is all I could ever hope for. I want you to be happy and make those around you happy. You have a special gift about you. One that the world will one day see, just like they will with Janet, David, and Thelma Louise. You are all special individuals, and your momma in her heart must be so dang proud of you all."

I had to wonder if she were right. Was Momma able to understand what we were contributing to this world? Did she know that Janet was about to start her master's degree, on the other side of the country, making a life for herself? Did she know that Thelma Louise had 2 beautiful children that did not even know who she was? Or that Davey, who was finally getting some playing time, would follow in her footsteps and also get an education so he, too, could do something bigger? I wondered a lot.

On the way out of there, Grammy decided it would be the perfect day to enjoy some fresh ice cream, and to sit on a bench in town, looking out at the cars and trucks driving past, the people heading into the stores in search of things they probably did not need, and just reflect. I thought that was the perfect plan as well.

We had a good morning thus far, learning about that little girl that had left so soon, so sudden, and I had a chance to talk with Grandad, feeling as if he was listening. It had been almost like he was there, in the flesh, sitting next to both Grammy and me on his stone. Maybe he had been, and we just could not see him. Maybe he was there beside us, laughing and smiling at the things we talked about, wishing he could go with us when we left. It was all so mysterious, and I decided to not think about it for the rest of the day. I wanted to be happy today. Davey would be calling after supper time, and Thelma Louise would be by in the morning with Natalie and Patrick. Grammy loved those days, getting on the floor, rolling a car around on the rugs, or pretending a tiny baby doll needed a diaper change. She lit up when Thelma Louise came by, and tomorrow was her day.

By the time we finished our ice cream, I had made a

tough decision, but I would not tell Grammy about it just yet. I first wanted to talk it over with Davey and get his advice. He would know exactly where I was coming from, and what I was feeling about it all. Baseball was probably just not for me. Not now, anyhow. I mean, Davey was ten times better than I was, and he was struggling just to get on the field. It bothered him some, but he knew there was a bigger purpose ahead for him, and he embraced that.

I overheard Grammy a week ago tell a friend that Davey may come back after school and coach the JV team at the high school. It would suit him well, I thought. He was liked by everyone, including the parents of the kids in town, and he knew the game inside and out better than most. If he could not play, he could certainly give back to the game he loved so much and coach. Davey had not told me any-thing yet, so I did not want to bring that up to him on my own. He told Grammy and no one else for a reason, and I would just wait until he told me. Besides, he had two years left before he graduated, and maybe things would change before then. Nothing was set in stone, and time would help lead him to where he was supposed to go, I figured.

As soon as we finished watching the folks go back and forth in and out of stores, Grammy said she felt the need to go home and rest. She had left a long week behind her, she explained, and just needed some time to unwind and do nothing for a short time. I gathered our things together and brought them over to Grandad's old but reliable truck, asking her if she was okay. She just waved me off and told me she was just fine, and not to worry at all. All she needed was a little time to rest and relax, or "R and R" as she liked to call it, and she would be right as rain.

Off we went, heading back home up the maple tree-lined road and over the lime green colored bridge out of town, to where we had seen so many people come and go. I looked once again out the pollen covered window on that short ride home and noticed all the changes around us. Millers Hardware had replaced their old rickety broken ceramic sign with a new colored plastic one with lights. Those 3 horrible looking homes that had faded gray asphalt shingles for siding on them just by the water, had been torn down now, and someone was planning to build three brand new homes in their place, complete with boat docks. Flowers were blooming wildly, and tiny black and yellow bumble-bees were buzzing around, and while that part would never change so much else was changing over time. I remembered all that Grandad had told me and wondered, where would I be twenty years from now, and what would Red Creek be like?

Chapter 17

Finding Sarah

* * *

By the time I hit seventeen, a lot had changed for our family. Janet was about to complete her master's program and was interning at a place called Mallard Associates Engineering, which was in Seattle. When she called and talked about all the things there were to do in Seattle, it sounded as if she would never have a desire to come back to Red Creek, except maybe for a visit here and there. The Seattle rain she quite enjoyed, and I could easily see why.

Janet loved everything about the rain. The music it made dancing on a tin roof, the smell of fresh falling rain on the front porch as it reached in and touched the stained wood planks. How it chased so many people inside, when she felt it invited her out. The rain was different for Janet than it was for others. Grammy said she was a hippie at heart when it came to things like that, but she meant it in a positive way. She knew Janet was a free-spirited animal, and things that others saw as an inconvenience, she found as opportunity. Janet was always talking about the fact that if we did not have the seasons changing, and the rain and snow were not a part of our lives, we would not have the flowers to grow, and die so new ones could rise in their place.

Time was different for flowers that lived and died over a single season, but they knew no better, so it was a span of life for them and they shined brightly for that time. Life for us was over several years for the most part, and that was our season to shine, she explained. Our season happened to be longer than it was for a marigold, but it was what it knew, so the flower shined during its time. As a marigold grows, it starts off as a seed, then becomes a seedling, and then expands upwards and outwards, until its flower blooms. When its cycle ends, and it eventually dies, it leaves a great bundle of seeds where its flower once was, and they drop off like raindrops, laying just on top of the surface of the soil over the winter, then slowly allowing the dirt to pull them in and cradle them, until the season where it starts the cycle over once again. That was how she saw the rain and snow. As essential to life, as much as it was to death.

Davey was graduating, and shortly would be moving back to Red Creek, to coach the JV team for the Red Creek High Sun Devils. He would still look for work, now that he would have his degree in Business Management, but his love of baseball, and his hometown, was strong and he would continue to be involved in his passion for as long as he could.

The funny thing was, that in his junior year, Davey saw

more playing time. He was not the standout star he had been while playing in high school, but he had a decent year. In one game, he went four for five, including hitting two home runs, one being the game winner, and that was the highlight of his college playing days. We were not in attendance, but thankfully one of the local stations had replayed the game, and we watched from the living room of Grammy's home. We sat, not unlike we did when the Reds won the World Series nine years back, expect that three people were missing. Davey looked so excited each time he swung that bat, and he was completely in the zone. Had he been able to do that over more games, maybe things would be different. But just a few games later, his hamstring gave him issues, and his playing time for the remainder of the year was severely limited. It would never get back to where it was, and he finished that year with only a few more total at bats.

Thelma Louise, well, she now had another child. A boy named Dustin Reynold, and Dustin was born several weeks early, like I had been. Only he would need to spend a month in the same hospital I was born at, until he gained enough weight that they could safely take him home. Mike, for his part, had been promoted to a regional manager, and that allowed them to move outside of town, just a few towns over from ours. He was maturing along with his career, and Grammy was proud, although she felt he should have done that long ago. Her saying was better late than never, and this was late, but it was not never. Plus, he had finally stopped trying to call her Grammy, and that went a long way with her. So long that when they came home with the baby to visit her, she had insisted that he now call her Grammy. He was utterly confused, but who was he to argue with her, especially after she had finally given him permission to call her what he had always done anyway.

Grammy, she was fine mostly, but father time was catching up to her some, and she was not as spry as she had been just even two years back. She was turning seventy-eight this year, and it was showing. Her memory was fading just a little, that if you were not paying much attention, you may not catch it. I caught it, though, because I had been with her alone for several years now. She would repeat things sometimes or ask the same question several times, but it was nothing to be alarmed about, I felt anyway.

She was still in charge of her life, and still drove into town almost daily. Grandad's truck was still running strong, and she called that faded red Chevy "Old Reliable." Because Grandad had taken such good care of it, she felt it had set a precedent and it would run well for her for years to come. That maybe the truck had a mind of its own, and knew it was well cared for and loved, and therefore would continue to thrive year after year. She was putting more miles on it in the last two years, more than before. Partially because she was always trying to stay busy and heading into town was the best way to do so.

I think Grammy felt that if she stayed still for too long, she was telling her body it may be time for her season to end, and she was nowhere near ready for that. The trips to see Grandad slowed down some for us, as I got more involved with my studies and hung out more with my friends on the weekends and spent less time with Grammy. She understood, but I am sure she was a little sad because I was her last one left in the house. Empty, it would not be the same, and she was not ready for that either.

Momma was still mostly the same, but with some new drugs on the market, they were trying things a little differently. It was never really told to us kids what had happened to Momma exactly, and I was not sure that it mattered. She would always be our Momma, and so whoever she was at the present, was not a reflection on who she was before. I saw her for the amazing, selfless person she had been in my early life, and so that was how I would always see you.

My trips to see Momma were now spaced out more though than they had been, and I felt pained about that. It wasn't that I did not care. Not at all. There were several reasons, actually. For one, it was hard to sit there for an hour and talk but hear no response. Grammy had reminded me this is exactly what I had done when we would visit Grandad, so she did not know why this was different for me. It was, though. With Grandad, I knew to never expect a true response. With Momma, I just kept hoping that eventually, one day, she would surprise us all and just respond, even if it was just the simplest of responses. I would settle for a sign she had understood anything I said at all.

The next issue was timing. We generally went on Saturdays because of classes, but lately, I had been hanging with friends more and more, and I just felt like I wanted to experience that time of my life and do the things young boys did. Grammy was also having more trouble on those long drives, and I was just finally driving Momma's old car, but that drive would still be a much longer drive than I was capable of doing just yet.

Meanwhile, I met a girl. I had met a few actually, but I began to focus on one in particular. Her name was Sarah, and she was the daughter of a doctor with a small practice in town. Sarah was great. She had a soft expression, and big dark brown eyes that seemed to take over her face. Her hair was down just past her ears and had just a slight wave to it. Being as shy as she was, it was a miracle we had even connected. I was a little shy too but was coming out of my shell more and more every day.

Fortunately, Grammy really liked Sarah too. In fact, she enjoyed her so much that she would always ask me when she would be over next and would often invite her for supper. She would remind me every time Sarah left, "Now don't you go and mess this one up, Jasper."

It was funny because, even still, Grammy was the only one to call me Jasper, and it took Sarah by surprise the first time she heard Grammy say it. It amused her, and she asked me where the nickname had come from.

"Honestly, I do not know. She told my momma when I was born that she refused to call me Ronnie and felt that I looked more like a Jasper. I really don't know why."

She never asked more about it. In fact, she never pressed me for more than I was willing to offer on any subject, which I liked. Especially when it came to Momma. It was hard talking about her and I did not have many answers to give. When she asked what was wrong with her, I just said she had a nervous breakdown. That was it, and we stopped talking about it. It wasn't that I was trying to be rude or attempting to hide anything. It was just that talking about it was hard for me and honestly a little embarrassing. This way she had an answer and would let it be.

Sarah and I had been dating for a few months when Grammy asked her if she would like to invite her parents over for supper one evening. I was floored. Never had I even had a girl over Grammy's house other than Sarah, and now, she was inviting her mother and father to have supper with us? What would we talk about? How would we ever be able to explain that my momma was living in a looney bin that was a full state away and had not spoken a word in over nine years now. They would think we were dysfunctional and that would be the end of Sarah and me for certain.

That was not what I wanted at all. Plus, Grammy was becoming a little more forgetful herself, and I was finding myself reminding her of even simple small tasks. She'd forget to turn off the lights in the evening, or shut the refrigerator door, or turn off the faucet after washing a dish. When we talked, she would often re-ask a question I had answered just a few moments before. If the Doctor and his wife were answering a question of hers, and three minutes later she asked it once again, they would know that she was having some issues, and on top of the whole Momma thing, I saw no way they would leave our home with a positive thought in their minds about who their fine little Sarah was seeing.

I had little say in the whole matter, however. Sarah answered Grammy with an enthusiastic yes, and it was set. The next Saturday evening, Doctor and Mrs. Tunney, and obviously Sarah, would be having supper with me and my grammy, and that was that. Now, Grammy and I had to talk about what to cook for this meal. Plus, the house needed a good cleaning. Grammy, of no fault of her own, had started to let the house go a little. She was having trouble keeping up on certain tasks, and when I would try to help, it would only upset her. She swore she would get to it just when she was feeling up to it, and things just naturally piled on top of things, until we wound up with not just regular cleaning, but time-consuming projects. It did not matter so much that the bedrooms, that had once been organized so well, were now piled high with boxes and bags. Grammy had taken to buying items in town she either thought we needed (we did not), or that she felt I might need if I headed off to school the following year and chose a school too far to commute.

That was actually what she wanted. For me to commute. She never gave me a guilt trip about it, but she mentioned several times that she felt it would save me money, that she could do my wash for me, cook for me, and that we would have each other for company on the weekends. I was already out most the day and nights on the weekends now, so I am not sure what difference it would make for me to stay at a local school. I would just be out most times regardless, but the idea of me still living at home made Grammy happy.

Sarah came over early that Saturday morning and asked me if I would like some help with getting supper ready. What she was really asking was if I needed help cleaning or moving things so we would all have a place to sit and eat supper. I took her up on the offer, and while Grammy was in town, we quickly moved what we could into Momma's old bedroom and made just enough room for the five of us to sit comfortably and talk, while having supper.

Sarah took to the kitchen and cleaned the dishes that had piled high over the week, then wiped the counters down so they actually shined again. As I helped, my heart sank. Here I was, being raised by my seventy-eight-year-old Grammy, who had sacrificed so much of her life, so many of her golden years, as they say, to give her grandchildren the life they would otherwise not have. She had worked her hands to the bone to help two of her grandchildren attend colleges away from home and pitched in to help Thelma Louise whenever she got in a pinch. For me, she was about to once again step in where she could, to ensure I was afforded the same opportunity as the others and attend a school of my choice.

Her beloved husband had left her sooner than a man should leave his wife and her daughter was struggling to find her voice and her sanity. Her other children barely came around, and when they did, they got on her for the condition of the house, telling her time and time again that she "ought to sell that old thing." But she would not relent and swore she would be buried in that house. It was not just some old worn-down house. It was her home. Where she had raised her children, and then her grandchildren. Where she had sat on the front porch with the love of her life, looking across the fields of wild grass swaying in the mid-summer winds. Where people had come and had left her life. It was not even a thought for Grammy. Her house was nearly all she had left, and to leave that behind felt to her like giving up on life. That was just how she saw it and there was no changing her mind.

As I looked around the house, this home of ours, I felt like a terrible person. My eyes filled with tears, and Sarah noticed.

"Ronnie, you okay? Is everything okay? Have I done something wrong?"

She had done nothing wrong. She had done something everyone else failed to do, including me. She had shown me with a simple mundane task, that I had failed Grammy, and that if I did not make it right somehow, someway, I was not worthy to be called her Jasper. She needed me, just like I had needed her all those years back, and she had given me her time. Her love. Her life. She sacrificed for me so much, for all of us really, and everyone had left, leaving her here as if they were simply done with her. It was not the intent of course, and Grammy certainly knew we all had to discover our own paths in life as well, but it hurt her still. She may not have told us, but it was apparent that Grammy was hurting.

"Sarah, listen, when we finish here, would you mind doing me a favor?"

"Of course, Ronnie, anything. What is it?" she said confused.

"I would like to go and visit with my grandad, but I would like for you to come with me. Is that weird? If it is, I understand. I just, well, I just would like for him to meet you, and I have some questions to ask him."

She knew Grandad had passed many years ago. Everyone knew, but she searched my face to figure out what I was asking her exactly and why, but then with no further hesitation, she smiled and nodded yes. She did not need a word, because her smile said enough, and it made me stop crying altogether. She came around the now cleaned counter, put her arms gently around my neck, and pulled me in for a long, caring hug, that left me feeling relieved. Relieved that I asked her to meet Grandad and that she agreed. Relieved that her parents were coming over that night and meeting Grammy. I knew that particular supper would either be a steppingstone on our path or a tragedy that might end us, but either way it would happen eventually, so why not get it over with. I was also relieved that I was gaining a better understanding of just what I should be doing, that I currently was not. A purpose of sorts, as Grandad put it. He always told me, "Find your purpose always, in every situation. It may change with time and circumstances, but it will always be there. You just need to find it."

We finished tidying up as quickly as we could, jumped in my car, and headed over to visit Grandad. I told her I needed to make a quick stop on the way over. When we were a few miles out, I pulled over to the side of the road, next to a field covered with long sweeping grass, swaying in the wind to a song that I could not quite hear, but the grass seemed to. There were purples and pinks and whites speckled all throughout that tall grass, and then there were the weeds. The dandelions. They were reaching up high, trying to peak over the grass for a few moments of undeviating sun. As I sat there, for the first time ever, I swore I could hear them singing. It was almost as if they were all in tune with one and other, and they were singing to the heavens a song only they were meant to sing. It was their music, their song, that rang proudly out over all the other flowers and grasses.

I had a brown bag with me, and when I opened it, there came out a small insignificant vase, but it was just perfect for its purpose. I held it in my hand for a moment, studying its lines, and curves. My fingers ran up and down the sides, and I wondered what flowers were worthy of this vase. We walked, holding hands over to the field, and Sarah said not a word. She leaned down and pulled different colored flowers from under her feet. First, a few purple ones, then a few light pink ones with white in the middle. Then she grabbed a few pieces of light-colored ornamental grass that went perfectly with the purple and pink in her hands already. She looked out a little further, her eyes scanning across the open field, and took a deep breath in. Before she rose to her feet, she grabbed three more items from the earth, and placed them with the others.

"There, will these do okay? I like the yellow of the dandelions. They just seem to go so well with the others. Almost as if they were needed."

She had no idea how needed they really were, or how

needed she really was at that moment, but I managed to smile, and hold in the emotions that filled by chest and throat.

"You could not have picked a more perfect bouquet if you walked this entire field," I told her with a smile. And it was true. How she understood just what I was doing in that field, and exactly what I needed, I may never know. It was easy to pick the flowers from where they had been growing all their time. After all, everyone loved flowers. Well, mostly everyone. But she had decided the grass and the dandelions were just as important as the pink and purple flowers, and that was exactly what Grandad thought. No, he knew. He knew that they were just as important as anything else we saw. It was safe to say he would like Sarah. That I was not even worried about. I was happy that he would get to meet her now. It was the perfect day and setting for such an introduction.

Chapter 18

Meeting Momma

* * *

As fate would have it, I enrolled in school at the very same place Momma had gone years back. Back when she was focused on securing a better life for herself and us kids. Those same heavy doors she once opened, scared and unsure of what was ahead, stood before me now.

Times were very different, and a lot had changed, like the colors of the entryway, and the layout of the front area where staff checked in the students and answered questions from nervous incoming freshman. The staff itself had changed quite a bit as well, and the old paper forms had been replaced with computer monitors. While much was different, the goals were the same. To guide young people, and a few older ones that had gone back to school like my momma had, to an education that would help shape them and their path in life.

Although I was a little nervous, I was nowhere near as nervous as she had been. I only had a summer off between classes. Momma had taken years off, worked a job and had young children to tend to at home. Even with all of that she still found the will to push through and get a degree as she knew she could.

My studies would be in Human Development and Family Science. Something over the past year had stuck with me, and settled deep within, and I knew that I should learn more about what made people the way they were. I wanted a greater understanding of why people acted and thought the way they did. Perspective became highly important in my own life and learning about it became my main focus. I hoped that through my studies I would learn to better understand all Grandad had taught me, and maybe I would gain insight into what my own Momma was going through and learn how to help her better.

Sarah was attending school in Ohio, studying nursing, which made sense considering her father was a doctor, and she had a natural desire to help those around her. Things were going well between us, and we continued our relationship long-distance, for she and I knew that we were in love. I felt that almost immediately when we first set eyes on one another, but after that supper a year and a half ago with my grammy and her parents, things progressed rapidly. Watching her work on Grammy's home to ensure I was not embarrassed and knowing she truly did not care what her parents saw at the same time, was amazing. Her picking the right flowers and weeds that morning we went to visit my grandad for the first time, had sealed the deal for me. She was exactly what I needed in my life, and she was mine. Each time we talked on the phone, I just felt more connected to her.

We got together on weekends, as she was several hours away from Red Creek. Conveniently however, she was only an hour from where Momma was living. So, each week without fail, she made the drive to Saint Mary's Hospital, which really was a strange name for a place that had no clergy anywhere in sight. Times had changed, and it was mostly younger women and men working the halls now. The drive was a bit longer for me, but I had a renewed excitement about making it weekly. For one, I was finally getting back into the routine of seeing Momma, and after a few months, it felt like she could feel I was there. I was still not certain she knew who I was, but I was feeling confident that the visits were doing more good than harm. That had been something I had used as an excuse to not visit with her, and I hated myself for that.

Another reason I was enjoying the trips more was that I was able to see Sarah. For the first few trips, she just drove and met me in the parking lot, gave me a kiss and told me to go and be with Momma. She would wait outside by her car and pass the time paging through her books or simply look-ing out to the valleys that shared shades of greens and grays against the sky. After maybe a half dozen trips, she asked,

"Ronnie, what would you think if I asked you to come up and meet your mother? I would not say anything but would just sit with you and with her. To grow a better understanding of what makes you the man you are would just mean so much to me."

She had such a way with words. A calm soothing way of explaining things in a positive way. As we grew closer together, not distance, nor my burdensome past, could slow down the stubborn nature of our desires. We had to know every detail of what our journeys had been, to fully understand where we were heading. All I wanted was to graduate, find a decent, honest job, and one day marry my Sarah. I knew in my heart she was everything I envisioned when I thought about what was coming in my life.

It reminded me of how Grandad felt towards Grammy. All those astonishing tales he told me over the years we had together, and how it was all I ever wanted. Just to have a small piece of what that man had with Grammy. She had meant more to him than anything else in the world. When she was having an issue, he was by her side. When she wanted time to herself, he would smile and give her the space she needed.

We as humans seem to improve on things with time. Innovation and invention improve the things that make up our everyday lives. But with love? I swear the older generations had that all figured out, and all we did was try to make it better by making a big mess of it all. They knew what it meant to sacrifice, and to truly understand that you were not the only one who needed something. They had a poetic way of loving each other, without the need for grand gestures or romantic sonnets. It was not the words that enabled their love to stand the test of time, but the quiet small actions, or sometimes lack of action, that they tenderly offered one another every day that allowed their love to stay true and strong.

Sarah enjoyed sitting and watching me talk with Momma. She had so many questions, but she simply waited for us to leave the halls before she asked any of them. Sarah was perfect like that. Without me having to say a word, she just knew it was not the time for questions in the room. Besides, she truly felt Momma knew I was in that room. I do not know why she felt she knew, but she said she just had a strong feeling that Momma was aware. That changed how I spoke with Momma. It made me want to give more of myself in those visits and tell her all about what had gone on in the last several years.

For a long while, our visits consisted mostly of hello's and how are you doing today's, and Janet sends her best from Washington. Now, I actually talked. I talked as if she were listening and as if she were asking her very own questions. Maybe she really needed to hear me tell her about the house or school, or the time I tried out for the team and quickly realized it was not for me. Maybe she needed to hear what I had for supper the night before or about a woman I met that changed my way of thinking. With Sarah right there, I told her.

"Momma, this is Sarah. You remember her from last time, right?" I began. "Anyway, Sarah goes to school not too far from here, and we come each and every Saturday to visit with you. I wish it could be more, but for now, it cannot be. I hope you understand, Momma. But just know, I love you. Davey sends his love. He will be here next week. He promised. Thelma Louise and even Mike are coming as well. Imagine that, Mike is coming. You remember me talking about him? Grammy laughs when she remembers him calling her Grammy and her telling him not to, and now she actually looks forward to it. How strange is that? Janet, Janet is doing so good. You would be so proud of her, Momma. She's finishing her master's, and she's met a really nice guy. He's Indian. Well, he's from Pakistan, so I think they are Indian, only not the kind that started Red Creek. His name is Behram, but we call him Benny. Last month Janet said she would be planning a trip back as soon as she could get away and she was excited to come and visit with you."

After a time, Sarah talked with Momma as well. At first, it was just a simple "Hello Mrs. McFarland," but then it became more about who she was, and where her family was from. She told Momma all about her nursing school, and how she was excited to help others as soon as she graduated. What Sarah did not realize, was that she was already helping others. She was, without even knowing it, quietly improving the type of person I was, and at the same time, she had made Momma feel at ease. It was almost like that time I swore I heard those dandelions in the field singing. Momma just looked different. She felt different. Almost as if she were trying to tell us something, trying to find her song, but she could not. I was just grateful for the time I spent with her, and for the small changes I saw occasionally. I felt that the more time we had spent in that hospital with her, the more she had a desire to break free of whatever was keeping her trapped inside herself.

I would drive back sometimes Sunday afternoon, but for the most part, I traveled in the late evening on Saturdays, arriving home early in the morning Sunday. The drive at that time of night was actually quite peaceful and gave me an opportunity to reflect on my time with Momma and Sarah and think about the future and my purpose on this earth. Time was becoming more of a friend than a foe, and I tried to use each moment I had as an opportunity to learn what would become my purpose, whatever that would be. Grandad said that purpose was something that was simply there, but that it was like a puzzle. We had to take all the pieces of our lives, from different angles and times, and combine them into one big picture, to truly understand our purpose.

He was smart and could see life so clearly, and I wondered if he had always been like that, or had it been a combination of losses and victories that shaped him into the man he had been. Maybe it was the Great War that taught him about himself, or maybe it had been that boy he had not intended to harm, dying all those years before. Maybe it was meeting the one woman that truly made him feel complete, or maybe, it was the combination of all of that. Had his life been easier, maybe he would not have been the man he was. When he said that if everything were easy, life would be boring, he was speaking words of wisdom I would not understand for a long time.

One morning after getting back early in the am, Grammy called me from the other room. I did not hear her at first because I was in a deep sleep, but on her third try, she got my attention, and I sat up, clearing my head, wondering what was going on.

"Jasper, Jasper, are you up?"

She sounded panicked, which was unusual for her. Wiping the crud from the corner of my eyes and still not able to open them freely, I replied,

"Yes, Grammy. Yes, I'm here. What's the matter?"

She waited a moment, as if she were trying to collect herself, or maybe she was searching for a way to let me know what was going on, without worrying me. She was always a strong woman and never wanted to need help from anyone. She needed me now though, and when I realized that, I quickly sprung from my bed, tossed the blankets and pillows off the side of the bed, and hurried into her room. When I reached her door, which was only two rooms away from mine, I saw Grammy in her bed, lying to one side, and in a position that did not appear to be comfortable or normal. She was struggling to turn towards me, and said she felt frozen in her spot. Not knowing what to do exactly, I asked her what she needed from me.

"Well, Jasper, I think it may be best to call 911. Just tell them I am some sort of stuck, and that if they come here, they should be able to help set me right."

I frantically ran to the other room and dialed 911. When they arrived at the house, a few of the newer neighbors had gathered out front of their homes, looking down to see what all the commotion was. Grammy was going to absolutely hate this senseless attention. She was fine, she had said and really did not want to go in the ambulance down to the hospital anyway. All she wanted was a swift kick in her backside to straighten her out. I had to tell her they did not kick old folks in their rears to straighten them out. Then I wondered to myself if they had ever done that, but I had no time to ponder on Grammy's funny stories.

I was on the phone with Sarah, explaining what was going on, and she told me it sounded as if Grammy was having a stroke. She would leave right away and drive all the way here. I told her she did not have to do that and that I would keep her posted. However, she simply insisted. The truth was, I was glad she was coming. I needed her here. Janet was far away, and Thelma Louise had been traveling with her husband and kids to visit his parents who had recently retired to Florida. Davey was close by, and I knew he would be heading over just as soon as I told him, but I wanted Sarah with me. I needed her.

"Okay, Sarah. Be careful, Okay? I'll see you soon. I love you."

Before she was loaded into her chariot, which is what Grammy called the ambulance, she asked me not to call anyone else. She did not want to worry anyone, and I reluctantly agreed. She was off and I told her I would be following right behind and be there when she arrived. The second the ambulance pulled off and down the street, with the sirens blaring in the early morning fog, I ran back in and dialed Davey's number. I may have promised her, but I did not want to deal with Davey wondering why I did not see the need to call him, especially if anything were to happen. He would kill me.

"Davey, it's Jas...I mean it's Ronnie. Grammy was taken to the hospital, but she swears she is alright. Just needing a kick in the rear. I spoke with Sarah, and she seems to feel like it may have been a stroke. I'm heading over there now and thought you might want to meet me there."

Davey was off the phone in a minute's time, dressed, in his car, and on the road. Not far from the hospital, he actually beat me and the ambulance there. When Grammy saw him waiting at the entrance to the emergency room, she started to cuss, but was having trouble because the one side of her mouth was drooped down still.

"A swift kick in the ass, huh, Grammy? I'll give you a swift kick," teased Davey.

When I got there, Grammy was already in the back, getting a set of tests to determine exactly what had happened. Davey was seated just outside the waiting area, leaning against a wall, and looked a little nervous. I walked over to where he was standing and punched him lightly in the shoulder.

"Hey, Davey."

"Hey, Squirt," he replied.

"How's she doing?" I asked casually.

"Dunno, they just took her back about ten minutes ago, and I'm waiting for the doctors to come out and let me know. When's that girlfriend of yours getting here, Ronnie?"

"It'll take her a few hours still. She was leaving her dorm and heading straight here. I guess maybe three, four hours?" I told him.

"Ronnie, if you do not marry that girl, I may start to tell

people you are gay. She's one of a kind, and what she sees in you, I may never know," he kidded. "Honestly, Ronnie, you guys are good together. You may never find another one like her, so be smart, you hear? Be smart. Listen to your big brother."

He was right, and although I already knew what he said was true, it really hit home in that moment. Sarah was always there for me whenever I needed her. She understood me and knew instinctively what I needed, sometimes even before I did. To try and find someone who could even hold a candle to her was simply a waste of time. I did not have a desire to meet other women while at school, and some of my friends teased me that I acted as if I were already married. They would rib me for not going to parties and trying to meet and hook up with random people, but I guess I was just a little different.

Maybe I was crazy, but I just felt like I was one of the lucky ones and met my soul mate at an early age. People went their entire lives struggling to find what I already had. It was so very wonderful and so simple. Sarah was my girl, and she was all the girl I needed. Besides, Grammy did not always like people from the start, but with Sarah, it was just instant. She knew how to read people and had read Sarah from the first minute. She reminded me several times, to not screw it up, and she was right. I could not let that happen.

Chapter 19

No Words Spoken

* * *

Sarah had grown up in a well to do family known throughout town as good, respectable folks. Her father had doctored many of the townsfolk, and had even been there for the births, and sadly, the death of others. Dr. Tunney had seen a lot in this small town, as many small-town doctors had. When things were too great for him to handle on his own, he would refer doctors from larger hospitals to assist in helping to diagnose conditions so a treatment plan could be effectively started. When Sarah called to tell him about Grammy, he immediately called the hospital to see what doctor was on call and headed over to meet him. It turned out to be a very close friend of Dr. Tunney's, and he felt confident that Grammy was in the best hands.

Sarah was correct. Grammy had indeed had a stroke. She suffered partial paralysis, losing the feeling in the left side of her body almost completely, as if it were not there any longer. She was fatigued and wanted to rest, and we allowed her to do just that. For so many years she had been on the go, trying to do so much for everyone else, and now, she needed to just lay, and rest, and heal. The doctors did not know if, or just how much of her left side she would regain, but they were hopeful. It would just take time to see. We had to be patient, and more importantly, Grammy had to be patient. That was easier said than done, but she was getting older, and she had just a little more patience than she once had.

While I spoke with Dr. Tunney, Davey called Janet, who knew how to reach Thelma Louise. Janet was on her way home, even though Davey told her there was nothing for her to do. Thelma Louise would not be able to get back just yet but would come in a day or so. Mike said he would put her on the next flight home, and he would join her at the end of the week. Everyone wanted to be by Grammy's side and felt a little selfish for not having spent much time with her lately. She had raised us, giving us a start and path on the very life we now all enjoyed, and we needed to give her all we could now when she needed us most.

By the time Sarah arrived, we were back in the room sitting beside Grammy. Davey was cracking jokes to lighten the mood in the room, and Grammy was trying to tell him to shut his mouth or else she would slap him silly. We were all laughing, including Grammy, who enjoyed the banter because it took the attention off her predicament. She hated attention, and Davey knew this all too well. It was good he was there because I had no idea how to make her feel calm, and he just had that ability to put people at ease. She probably really did want to slap him silly after a while, but it was all in good fun and done with love. The McFarlands had overcome a lot in our lives, but we were tough for it and we knew how to find the positives in even the worst situations.

When Sarah walked in, I was mentally exhausted. My entire body was tired straight down to the bone, and my mind was spent from trying to figure out how I would handle all this. It was clear Grammy would need much more attention and help while she recovered, and if she did not, God forbid, recover, what then?

I had school, a part-time job at a pizza joint in town delivering in the evenings, and I had Sarah and Momma who needed our Saturday visits. Sarah was in a school, hours away, and while we handled our relationship exceptionally well all things considered, it was not easy by any means. If I had to stay here and could not visit her there, I wondered what would happen to us. Sarah would have trouble getting to Red Creek to see me since her school load was a lot heavier than mine, and she had taken on a part-time job at a hospital near her school to break herself into the field quicker. I loved that about her. How dedicated she was to what she wanted to do for a living. It was so much more than a job to her though. She truly loved the thought of helping people with their ailments. Watching people put their complete trust in good doctors and nurses and entrusting themselves to their care always made her ponder if medicine was her calling. There is no doubt it was. People liked her mannerisms, her warm smile, and how quickly she put those around her at ease with just a few words. It is what first attracted me to her.

When Grammy saw Sarah, she reached out with her right hand to motion her over to the side of the bed. Her eyes were focused on Sarah, but her words would not leave her mouth, no matter how hard she tried to will them out. It did not matter. Sarah knew. She knew without Grammy having to say a word, just how she felt, and what she wanted to tell her. Sarah held her hand with one of her own, and with the other, she touched Grammy's cheek, smiling warmly at her. Grammy's eyes filled with tears, and Sarah quickly wiped them away. She told her she was so happy to be back in her company, and that as soon as she was up and around, ice cream was on us. That made Grammy smile as best she could with only one side of her face able to form a curl, and the room was silent.

Davey put his arm around my shoulder and leaned in.

"Ronnie, you better put a ring on that one, or somebody else will."

It made me feel so happy that everyone loved her, and I loved her. I loved her. As often as I had said that to her, I felt in that moment, just how powerful that was. I did not want to spend a moment without her in my life. This woman had made my entire family look differently at me. That spoke volumes about the type of person she was. You can fake certain patterns of your personality, but you cannot fake who you are. She was absolutely magnificent.

At that moment, the doctor walked swiftly into the room and asked how we were all doing. He said hello to Sarah and smiled, telling her that her father had just stepped out on a call, but that he wanted her to stop by home before she left back for school. She nodded in agreement, and without looking, took her free hand and placed it on mine, while still holding on to Grammy's.

"So, Millie, you had a stroke as I am sure you are aware by now," he started.

Funny, I had forgotten her name was Mildred, and people called her Millie. So many people called her either Grammy or Mrs. McFarland, that it slipped my mind all these years that she had a real name. I found this amusing, but with the seriousness of the conversation, I planned to smile and laugh about that a little later. Probably over a beer with Davey.

"You are showing signs of improvement already, but it may not be a quick turnaround for you, so you are going to need to be patient. We are optimistic that you will regain at least most of your control back, but again, it's just too early to give you a promise of that."

I asked a few questions about how long she would need to stay in the hospital, and what would be required when she got back home. He was vague on what would be required, other than that she would need physical therapy a few times a week to help her improve the use of her arm and leg, but that she could be released in just a few days if she felt up to it. Oh, she would feel up to it all right. She hated being there. Everything about being in a hospital bothered her. I do not know if she had been to one in her entire life, to be honest. If she had, other than when

Grandad was there, she never mentioned it.

So, the plan was, at least for the time being, that Davey and I would alternate times watching Grammy in the evening, and Thelma Louise and Janet would take days, at least until Janet had to go back to Washington. Her job had given her leave, but only for a short time. The understanding was that Janet would arrive back home sometime on Monday, and Thelma Louise more than likely tomorrow evening. That gave us all a few days to prepare the home for Grammy to return. We had to make room for her to walk without all the obstacles in the way. Dishes would be lowered to the bottom shelves for ease of access. Her bed would be placed in the living area, so she would not have to walk far for much. Davey planned to build a ramp during the week out of wood, so she could be pushed in a wheelchair if need be. That thought bothered the heck out of me. I was unsure if Grammy could mentally grasp that she may need a wheelchair to get around. She was the proudest woman I knew, so that would be a long shot. She may allow us to give her piggyback rides before she saw herself pushed around in a wheelchair.

Sarah headed on down to the cafeteria and grabbed some sandwiches for Davey and me, and a wrap for her. I had not realized that we had not eaten all day to this point, and it was late afternoon now. Come to think of it, I did not feel overly hungry. I guess being consumed by what was going on had taken control of my hunger as well.

"What time do you need to go back, Sarah?" I asked, taking a big bite of my tuna salad on rye she brought back.

"Back? Not today. Ronnie, I will stay a few days and help out. I am not going back right now. You need me here," she replied, almost as if she were shocked, that I had asked that question at all.

"I just meant, well, I figured you would need to get back before classes started, that was all. Of course, we are grateful for your help, Sarah. That is very kind of you," I said back peddling trying to not sound as if I were not.

"Extremely grateful, Sarah. Thank you." Davey added.

Sarah smiled and just said, "Then that is that."

She went back to sitting by Grammy, and started to talk to her about the weather, and how different it was in Ohio, which was just a state away. She told Grammy about her studies as a nurse, and all she was learning while there. Grammy just looked at her and nodded as she listened intently. It was clear the bond these two women had created, and I could not be happier. The difference in years between them did not matter. It was almost as if they were old friends who had known one another much longer than Sarah's age would have made possible, and were simply catching up after a time away.

Over the next day, Sarah, Davey, and I spent most of our time tirelessly scrubbing floors, and toilets and counters, taking out trash bag after trash bag, and cutting the high grass, careful to leave a few dandelions for Grammy to fuss over. We changed out some of the old dim light bulbs for brighter white ones and moved her bed out into the living area. Davey brought over a bigger television set, so she did not need to struggle so much to watch her shows.

While we were attending to all those chores, the doorbell rang, but we were not expecting anyone. We looked at each other, knowing that Janet wasn't due until late that evening, and Thelma Louise was still a day away. Davey was closest to the front of the home, so he put down the trash bag he had in his hand and walked over to the door to see who it may be. As he looked through the screen door, he could see who it was clear as day. It was Doctor Tunney and his wife. They explained to Davey they had come over to see what they could offer in the way of help. As Davey opened the door to welcome them in, Sarah ran up and gave a warm hug to both of her parents. She knew they were coming all along but allowed them to be the ones to surprise us with the news. It was perfectly done and caught both me and my brother off guard. They were really good folks, but I never could have expected them to show up on my front porch with an offer to help us get things ready for Grammy. Being at the hospital was one thing, as he had more than one reason for being there, but this? This was the type of thing you did for family.

We ordered a few pizzas, cracked open a two-liter bottle of Pepsi, and found some clean glasses for each one of us. Then, we sat down and ate. As we sat there, just talking about what we had planned for the room, the house, and for Grammy overall, Doctor Tunney asked if he could talk with me in private. Now, we had talked several times over the past few years that Sarah and I were dating, and even a few times in private, but this felt different. I was a little bewildered about what he might want to talk about, but whatever it was, I was willing to listen. So, I put down my pop, walked out to the front porch, and together we walked to the side of the house, away from everyone else. He placed a hand on my shoulder as we stood side by side and looked directly at me as he spoke.

"Son, I wanted to talk with you in private, just you and me. I know you have a lot going on in your life right now, and that with your grandmother coming home soon, things are going to get even a little more hectic for you and your family. Before all of that hits, I needed to tell you something. I'm proud of you, Ronnie. I know I am not your dad, but I know that somewhere, he regrets not being a part of your life. If he doesn't, well, it really does not matter. You have come from a place where so many people never get out of. They get stuck, spin their wheels, and find every excuse to fail. No one would blame them for that. But you? You have used your past as a reason to succeed. A reason to work harder, and a reason to inspire others around you. What you have been able to do with so much heartache is nothing short of astonishing. Your grandmother is a special woman, who happens to have four very special grandchildren, including you. Sarah, she loves you, and I know you love her. Whatever may happen between you two is your business, but I want you to know, I think of you as a son."

I was frozen, and just so caught off guard that I had no idea how to respond, so I just looked up at him, and thanked him. He smiled, knowing I was unsure where he was going, and with how to respond to something that was so out of the blue.

"Ronnie, that evening you invited us over for supper with your Grandmother, Sarah came home and was in tears. She walked in and fell into my arms, crying like I had not seen her do in many years."

"Why was she crying, sir?" I asked.

"She was crying because she felt that you had worked so hard for all you had, and still felt it was not good enough for her, or her family. That you had tried so hard to impress us and felt embarrassed about what you had to offer her and by your surroundings. She mentioned about going to speak with your Grandad that morning and stopping to pick up those flowers to leave for him. She also told us about your mother and that you had gone to visit her as much as you could, and how much that affected you as a person. What I am trying to say to you is, from the first night we had supper with you and your grandmother, Ronnie, we knew you were special. We could tell you had a heart bigger than most, and that your intentions were good. We can't say that for many people, but you, well, you made an impact on us that evening. You made a strong impact on Sarah that evening, which is the reason she tries to give so much of herself to you. She loves you, and that says something. Treat her right, Ronnie. Treat her fair. She will always do more in return."

At this point, I was emotional, and full of confusion. When they left that night after supper, it had never come up again. Sarah never told me about going home and crying, nor did she mention how her parents felt about me. That was how she preferred it. I think she enjoyed watching things unfold organically, only when they were meant to happen as fate would desire. She preferred for her father to tell me how he felt at just the right moment. There could be no better moment than now, and he knew that. She knew that. I needed this, and here it was, this heartfelt sentiment shared by the most unexpected, and yet somehow, the most expected, person.

Dr. Tunney pulled me in a little closer, and gave me a half hug, as if he were unsure how I would react to a full-blown hug. It was just fine. Either was just fine by me. We walked back inside, and before I hit the door, I wiped at my eyes to make sure there were no tears forming. That was all I needed Davey to see. Although somehow, I felt he knew what was going on outside. Davey read people well, and this was maybe easier for him to read than it was for me.

That night, we finished clearing out most of the downstairs, and things looked pretty darn good if you asked me. Grammy's bed was ready, and we added some extra-long curtains so she would have more privacy. The new television was all set to go, and we filled the pantry and refrigerator with groceries. As we sat back to relax, I looked around the room at everyone. They were just sitting there, feeling proud of what they had accomplished that day. They had every right to be proud, I had not seen the house look so well put together since, well, since all three of my parents were living in it. Back when Momma, Grandad and Grammy all sat around the living room just as we were in that moment. I was proud. Proud of who had helped. Proud of what we had accomplished. Proud of how I was raised by those three incredible people.

A little later a car pulled up out front of the house, and we all expected to see Janet with her bags, but instead, it was Thelma Louise. Thelma Louise had flown in on an earlier flight, not sleeping at all, and came straight to the house to be with her family. When she walked in the front door and dropped her bags, I ran over and gave her a big hug. I had not seen her in some time and missed my sister dearly.

"Ronnie, hey. I missed you too, little brother. I missed you too."

We just needed Janet to arrive that evening, and we would once again all be in the same room, for the first time in many years. That reunion had taken way too long, but I was happy that it was going to happen while Grammy was still alive. She needed it. We all needed it. Life was going to be okay.

Chapter 20

The Wedding

* * *

As the weeks and months passed, the warm weather turned cold, and the cold back to warm. Seasons stopped by, and then after a short visit, left just as fast, as if to remind us they each existed and didn't want to be forgotten. It was time's way of moving forward without hesitation, and it reminded me that to wait for tomorrow was pretty much the same as giving up. Time did not care what I thought of her. She just continued marching on at her own steady pace. Never speeding up, and never slowing down. She could be arrogant that way and did not care what we thought or needed from her.

Grammy spent the next several years working on herself. It was incredible to me that it was taking years to recover what she had lost that fateful morning, over the short course of time it would take to drink a simple half cup of coffee. She did not regain full control of her left side, however, she was able to get along with what she did get back, and she made the best of it. While her physical strength and abilities returned, her mind grew a little fuzzy and she lost track of dates, and what show she had just watched on the television, and even sometimes if she had had breakfast that morning or not.

Davey was a huge help over those few years. He decided to move even closer and rented a home just a few blocks from where we lived. He continued to coach ball, but also landed a better position in a place just north of Red Creek. Davey lived on his own and rarely had a steady girlfriend. When he did, it usually fizzled out quick and he'd find himself as a bachelor once again, which was just fine by him. He liked his freedom, and being a good-looking fit guy, never had trouble finding something to do on a Friday night.

Janet and Benny's relationship continued to evolve, and she began planning her wedding. After giving it some serious thought, she decided to do the wedding back home in Red Creek, with just close family in attendance and a modest reception. They would then go back to Seattle and enjoy a larger reception amongst their friends and Benny's family there. Benny had been out on a few occasions with her, when Janet had flown in to check on Grammy and to visit with Momma.

The good news was that we took Momma out sometimes for a few hours during the past year, and Grammy loved that. Davey and I would help Grammy get into the car, and in true Davey fashion, he would ask her if she needed a swift kick to help her into the car. Grammy would always respond with,

"Davey, I'm about to swift kick you out of this life in a second."

It was great. Having her back as close as we could to who she was, meant a lot to all of us, and I think Davey being around closer was instrumental in all of that. When I was busy with school, or traveling out to visit with Sarah, he would swing by and pick her up to visit Grandad on Saturday mornings before his games. Sometimes it was early in the morning, and that was simply fine by them. Few folks were up yet, and they had the entire cemetery to themselves. Grammy would just sit there most times and talk with Davey about this and that, but it was the fact she was close with Grandad that was most important to her. Davey told her one of these days he would find her a nice old man with one foot in the grave to take care of her, and Grammy would just call him a jackass. They had built a powerful bond between them, and it was so good for them both, even if it was a little unconventional.

"Grammy, can I ask you something?" Davey asked her on one of those brisk early fall mornings. The leaves were falling on the ground around the base of the stones, and they both had light winter coats on, with Grammy in a knitted green hat.

She did not respond, but that just meant that he could go on, and he would have anyway regardless, and she knew that.

"All those drives that Ronnie did with Grandad, and all the trips into town for ice cream sitting on that old bench. What made Grandad so partial to Ronnie? I mean, he was good to us all, but with Ronnie, it just seemed as if there was something different between them. I'm not complaining, just curious about that is all. What was it about Ronnie, that just made Grandad see him in a different way?"

Grammy was bundled up, her arms resting on her stomach, looking at the stone with Grandad's name and dates inscribed deep into the surface. The stone had lost some of the luster it once had because of the seasons changing back and forth, and some green moss had found its way into the crevices of the words. Grammy always refused to clean it out. She felt that Grandad would appreciate the dark-colored soft moss, just as he did the weeds, because it must have some purpose, even if we could not understand what it was. She imagined he was looking down, smiling because she just left things as they were, and allowed that moss to grow there, undisturbed.

"David, Jasper needed just a little more from him. Grandad was able to read people well, and he knew that you and your sisters were strong and had what was needed to navigate this world without needing a lot of direction. You were tough-skinned and had a lot of friends, and Jasper was just trying to keep up. He wanted so bad to be like you..."

She trailed off, almost losing her place in the conversation and slurring some. Davey saw this and decided not to ask anything further. He just put his arm around her neck, leaned his head into hers and told her as he kissed her gently on her head,

"It's alright, Grammy. Spend time with Grandad. He's here with us, I feel it. Let's just enjoy his company, okay?"

Grammy looked a little confused at the fact her Walt was somehow there but yet not, and she looked down at her cold, shriveled hands, struggling to gain a grip on each other. Things had changed and she knew that but had no idea how or why.

On the day of her wedding Janet looked absolutely gorgeous. She wore an off-white dress that came to just past her mid-thigh. It had a few sequins along the bottom that caught the sun's light and sparkled whenever she turned, and she looked anything but plain. My sister was radiant as she stood up next to the man who would soon be her husband and recited her vows. I was thrilled for Janet, because she deserved happiness in her life, and I hoped that the joy I saw on her face and Benny's that day stayed with them through their marriage. Janet and I were very close despite her living so far across the country and away from her family, but she somehow made it feel like she was always just a few minutes away. I missed her immensely, but she made an effort to call, and the sound of her voice was always soothing and comforting. I admired her, looked up to her and the life she was building, and hoped that one day Sarah and I would find the same type of happiness.

Benny looked just as happy in his light gray suit, bright yellow tie, and dark gray handkerchief in his left breast pocket. His hair was neatly pushed to the side, and he kept things to the left for his bride. Janet did well to control some of her urges to keep all things left, but Benny knew his bride and recognized that wedding days are full of anxious details and wanted to do what he could to make this day as stress free as possible for her. His efforts did not go unnoticed by those of us who knew and loved Janet.

The best part of the day was that Janet got married on the Pennsylvania side of the Ohio border, so we were able to bring Momma for the ceremony. Davey left early that day to pick her up. I felt like he wanted that time alone with Momma, so I stayed behind and helped with whatever last-minute tasks were needed. Momma wore a maroon-colored dress with black flats and her hair was done by one of the nurses back at Saint Mary's. Everyone in attendance felt pure joy over seeing Momma sitting there, looking straight ahead, and wondered if she knew how far her children had come since she had gone away. She may not have been done up at a spa as other mothers were on their daughter's wedding day, but she looked absolutely magnificent to us. I was proud of Momma that day. Maybe she had not known where she was or what was going on, but maybe, just maybe she had. It did not matter, though, because her being there, in and of itself, was all that mattered to us. For the first time in many years, all the McFarlands were together in one town, and in one room.

Janet kept her last name, and in Benny's culture, that was a practice he was familiar with and accepted. The name did not matter as much as the union to him, and that made him okay in our family's eyes. He was a decent man, hardworking, and clearly looked at Janet the way Grammy had looked at our Grandad. That was a sign of a strong love that time and life could test, but that would not easily be broken.

Grammy wore a dark green suit jacket with gold accents along the sleeves, and green pants that fell not nearly close enough to her shoes. She had her soft white hair done up, and Sarah had dressed her skin with shades of beige and brown makeup so as not to be too flashy or take away from who she was. Grammy was a simple plain woman and preferred to not alter herself too much when possible. She sat next to Momma and used her good hand to hold Momma's and smiled. Those two women had lost a sense of time and understanding, but they were mother and daughter, and I refused to believe they did not know that with every fiber in them.

The entire ceremony, which lasted no more than twenty minutes, was attended by just two dozen people, including Dr. and Mrs. Tunney, but the size was somehow perfect for the day. The sun shone down brilliantly on the guests, and the mildly cold day felt unseasonably warmer. The grass was still green but appeared heavier at that time of year, slumping over as it struggled for the last bit of summer it could find, and the white, brittle dandelions were ready to die off in order to give life to more in the Springtime when their circle of life would repeat again.

After the ceremony concluded, we gathered in the hall where tables were set up in brilliant colors of yellow-gold, red and shades of green that brought some of Benny's hometown to rural Pennsylvania. The food was simple. Just an option of a fish dish or chicken, and sides of country vegetables with biscuits slathered in butter and jams. Glass champagne flutes were abundant and filled with golden sparkling wine. Music was played in the background, but they had decided not to do any traditional introductions. For them, it was a simple reception to celebrate two simple people who had fallen in love and were just adding the words Mr. and Mrs. to their names. It was a celebration, bringing good people together, who may never find themselves in the same room again.

Janet knew Grammy was growing older, and Momma, though improved slightly, seemed too far from who she once was to ever be the person she had dreamed of becoming. She watched as Grammy and Momma sat at their table, looking lost, but there still, right where they belonged. It was bittersweet to see the two of them like that, and Janet needed to leave the room to collect herself for a moment.

I followed her to the long hallway she snuck out to, and from ten feet away, looked at her as she tried to compose herself.

"Sis, thank you," I said to her.

"For what, Ronnie, what did I do?"

"So much. So much that I could never possibly thank you properly or explain just how I feel. You were always there for me, and I know you will always be. The way you allowed me to understand my childhood better. How you knew when I needed a distraction in life, and when I needed questions answered. For today, and how you moved everything out here for your day, so that Momma could be here, and Grammy could sit beside her daughter for the first time in a normal setting. Momma is proud of you, sis. I can tell. She may not show it, and may not be able to tell you that, but she is proud. More than you and I will ever understand."

She smiled my way, and put her hands over her mouth, then looked straight at me and took the steps needed to reach me where I stood. She put her arms around my neck and stared at me for a brief second, then hugged me like she never had before.

"Oh, Ronnie, you do not know how much that all just meant to me. I always tried to be the best big sister I could. I know it was not easy growing up as you did, but we came out such better people because of it, don't you think?"

"I do, sis. I do. We are McFarlands, and we know how to push through anything thrown in our way. Grandad told me that. Nothing could stop us, but us. If we had enough will, we could accomplish anything. Well, expect for baseball. That, I could just not do," and I laughed.

Janet laughed as well, still holding me close to her. When she finally let go, she smiled wildly and said,

"Let's get back in there. We have some dancing and celebrating to do. It's time to see those Ronnie moves in action," and she winked. Just like Grammy had always done.

When we walked back in, Benny, who had been talking with Sarah and her parents, looked over as if to ask if everything was okay, without actually asking. I smiled and just nodded to let him know all was alright. He smiled in return because he understood as men often do. He walked over towards Janet, held out his hand, and asked her if he could have this dance. She smiled, looked at the DJ, and the music started.

The song they danced their first dance as a married

couple to was "Forever Young." It made me think back to all I had seen in my twenty-plus years of life. How time, although sometimes patient, could also be cruel. How we thought Grandad had so much time left, but really, he did not. How Momma had a lifetime of lessons trapped inside of her, unable to share them with us. How Grammy was growing slower and steadily declining, and it was not fair.

Time did not care about right or wrong. Fair or unfair. She only cared to move at her pace, and no matter how hard we tried to slow it down, it never did. The one thing we had to accept was that in the end, we were all going to eventually leave this place, and a small piece of us would remain behind for as long as people remembered who we were. I wanted the piece of me I left behind to be special, and felt it was time to figure that part out, because time was not going to be patient for me.

Chapter 21

Eight Dandelions

* * *

Sarah and I finished earning our respective degrees, and she was back working in town at the same hospital I had been born at all those years back. That was exactly what she wanted to do with her life, and she had accomplished that for herself. I was working a job in editing that I had stumbled on by chance, but the truth of it was that I had bigger plans in store for my future. During the last two years, I had been working on an outline that would allow me to be a type of motivational speaker, and to give back to others from the lessons I learned through my journey in life thus far. Sarah told me if I did not pursue it then I did not understand just what Grandad had meant by "Purpose."

"Ronnie, this is your purpose. I am certain of it," she told me emphatically.

I began making small appearances and tailoring my presentations to the particular audience. A church in town asked me to speak on the subject of overcoming grief, and so I spoke from my personal experience on that. When a local divorce group heard how well that had gone, they asked me to come up with something for adults suffering through the hardships of separation, and impending divorce. I sat with Sarah, and we came up with an outline that included my life growing up, never knowing who my birth father was, and how my mother had struggled, but managed until she had come down with her sickness. I told the people in that particular group that although life was hard and threw so much at us, it was always adjusting and allowing us to change paths and directions. We were never stuck on one path but had some control over the direction we were going to travel from any point in life forward. When I was asked to return to that group a month later, I researched more and interviewed with folks who had both gone through divorce blindly, and ones who had known for a long time that it was what they wanted and had planned for. There was a massive difference in how the two groups processed their divorce experience, so I learned to draw from other people's experiences and incorporate them into my speeches so that everyone was able to gain from my perspectives.

The work was harder than I anticipated, but it was exactly what I wanted for Sarah and me. A path to something greater than the one I was previously on. If I could just change direction a little here and there, perhaps I could really do something with it, and begin to speak for larger groups, on varying topics, and be able to help even more people to understand hope, perspective, and purpose. It was important to see this through, and Sarah was backing me with all she had.

Sarah. I had been so busy with building this new venture, with seeing Momma as much as I could, and with helping Davey still with Grammy, that I had not taken the time to figure out what it was Sarah wanted out of life. I realized, beyond nursing I did not know what her plans and dreams and hopes were. I felt horrible, and so I planned a date for the two of us, in a restaurant that had just opened in Hillside, which was a forty-five-minute drive from our apartment. I told her to get dressed, we were going out. We had made it a habit to go out at least once a month. It was a part of our routine and we tried to use that time to forget about the difficulties in our lives, and just enjoy being together. I had to make two quick stops that morning, and then we were going to meet at the restaurant at five forty-five for our reservations. She was confused as to why we were not driving together, but I explained I would be coming from the other side of town and it just made more sense to meet.

When we arrived, I had a bouquet of flowers for her, already sitting on the table. In the bouquet were petite purple flowers, little pink and white ones, along with some light green ornamental grass. I had added 8 dandelions into the mix, and when she saw it, she immediately cried. It was the same setup she had picked those years before, to leave by my grandad's stone when they first met. Pulling out her chair, I grabbed the napkin off the table, seated her, and placed the napkin on her lap. I then gently pushed the chair in as she shifted to meet the table. Once seated myself, I asked her if she knew what the significance of the flowers were. She knew it had to do with the bouquet we made for Grandad because that had been such a very meaningful moment in our life, but that was all she knew. I asked her to count the dandelions, and so she did.

"Eight," she responded, confused.

"Yes, there are eight," I replied with a smile.

"Ronnie, is there a particular reason there are 8 of them there? I am sorry I'm not understanding."

"Sarah, my family means everything to me. Everything. I was always involved with them and grew to love them more than life itself. My Grandad and Grammy taught me so much, and while Grandad is gone, he still is teaching me lessons about myself. Grammy, although older and slower, is still one of the wisest people I know. I love Momma, although, she is not the person she once was, she is always my mother, and that will never go away no matter what happens. My brother and sisters have been there for me through so much, and honestly, without them, Sarah, I am not the person that sits here before you. These dandelions represent each of my family members, that have guided me, strengthened me, and believed in me. They may be imperfect to some, as a weed often is, but they have purpose just the same and are perfect to me."

I then allowed the waiter to pour our water, and he brought over a bottle of champagne in a pail of ice, opened it, poured a glass for each of us, and then placed it back in the ice.

"Ronnie. That is the sweetest thing I have ever heard. I know your family means more to you than anything else possibly could. I've known that about you from the first time we met. You wear your heart on your sleeve, and I admire that about you. People know what they are getting from you, all the time, Ronnie. But, Ronnie, there are eight dandelions. You mentioned each was for a family member that has made a tremendous impact on who you are. Who is the eighth representing?"

As she was speaking, I stood and walked over to her chair. She looked up at me, and I lowered myself down to one knee, removed a small black case from my left pocket, and opened it. Inside was a one caret round stone, with three smaller diamonds on each side. It was what I could afford at the time, and I had used all the money from my speaking engagements to purchase it. Sarah looked stunned, as if I had caught her completely off guard and she had not seen this coming.

"Sarah, you. You are my eighth dandelion. I mean, if you will just say yes. I love you, Sarah, and from the very first moment we met, I knew there was no one else for me. My life changed when you entered it, and you have impacted me just as my family has. So Sarah, I am asking you to join my family, and marry me."

She was crying now, holding her hands over her eyes, trying to not mess up her makeup that was now running all down along the sides of her face. She looked into my eyes, and responded,

"Yes. I thought you were never going to ask."

On the way to the restaurant, I had stopped by to see Sarah's parents. They gave me their blessing several weeks ago, but I wanted to drop off some flowers for her mom, and to thank her dad once again, before heading over to get the ring. On the way to get the ring, I stopped off at the same place she had picked the flowers for Grandad and looked out over the field. It was different now, but still, I could see just off the side of the road, those same vibrant colors she had once seen. As I picked the flowers from their place in the soil, I thought about how they would replenish themselves again and again, and feed life off to more down the line. It made me smile thinking about the time she and I stood there together, and how without a word, she knew exactly what flowers to choose.

After that, I stopped off at Grandad's to sit and talk with him for a few moments. I told him about the ring I had picked out, and how beautiful it was going to look on Sarah's tiny hand. Looking over to where that mother had once sat, talking to her little child that had passed at the age of only two days, I wondered what had become of her. She had not been back at the same time I was there visiting Grandad, but I was sure she had been there just the same. There were usually fresh flowers laying on the little girl's headstone, so I assumed her mother had stopped by when she could. Life went on for the ones still living it, and time stood still for only the ones who departed. They had no life left in them, no breath to give, but they had left behind lessons for us all if we just sat and listened for a while. I listened. That day, I sat and just listened. I felt Grandad tell me he was proud and that was all I ever hoped for. Leaving his resting place, I felt a sense of understanding I had not felt to this point.

After I grabbed the ring from the jeweler, I stopped off at the restaurant an hour before Sarah arrived, to order the champagne, and to leave the flowers on the table where we would be eating. The host had looked strangely at me, for the bouquet was not a typical one you would expect to see as the centerpiece on an upscale restaurant table, but I did not pay her any mind. There was no better centerpiece I could imagine, and so that made it the perfect choice for the occasion. I knew Sarah would understand the meaning behind it. I knew the emotions she would feel when she saw the bouquet. I knew before she even arrived. I knew my Sarah. More than myself almost. She was everything I needed in a partner, and she had made herself mine. All along I had her, but now, I would build with her. A family, just like I had growing up. Sisters and brothers who loved each other and who no matter what they faced, would overcome anything together. We were stronger together than we were on our own, and we all knew that. Each of us had a gift, and together those gifts were shared over a lifetime of growing.

Over the next year, we moved back to town, and found an apartment closer to Grammy, but still a place of our own. I was traveling a lot more now as my endeavor was taking off like a wildfire. It was getting to where it was hard to schedule anything shorter than six months out, and I was feeling the need to be home just a little bit more.

My Grammy was there. My brother Davey was there and my fiancé, who supported me wholeheartedly was there. Traveling had been exciting at first, but after a while the hotel rooms all blended together. The destinations all felt the same, and I was growing tired of eating alone every evening.

I was calling home every chance I had, and still more, larger groups of people were reaching out, trying to get me to speak at their events. Each felt my speaking style was exactly what their group needed. Being able to help people was what I wanted, and now, here I was, a sought-after motivational speaker, but I was run down. The pace of my schedule was grueling, and I decided to take a break for at least a month. I wanted to be home and to stay home for a few weeks with my family. Running myself down would be no good for anyone, so it was rest or suffer, and ultimately fail at what we had worked so hard to build.

Sarah was happy with my decision, and in her true fashion, she kept encouraging me, no matter what I wanted, or felt we needed. Her job had kept her busy as well, but she had also taken a role in helping Grammy more. She knew Davey was doing much of it on his own, and he too, was needing a break. So, with me gone, she would come home and relieve Davey, and spend the nights there with Grammy.

Grammy was not doing so well, and approaching her ninetieth birthday, we were becoming painfully aware that she was nearing the end of her time with us. She was now lying in bed all day, not able to drive, not able to swing on the porch any longer and had grown entirely unaware of who anyone was. It was sad to watch her as she struggled in her mind, to bring words to her lips, but they just did not want to come.

There were no longer trips into town to get an ice cream cone. In fact, that place had closed a few years back, and she never even knew. She could no longer get over to see Grandad, and at times would mumble things as if she were seeing him right in front of her. She would smile and chuckle at nothing, or maybe there was something. Something that only she could see. Maybe she was looking into her past, at a time that had long since left us, but had not left her. Her mind allowing a memory to be her reality again when she needed something most. Maybe she was looking into the future, to a time when she would be reunited with Grandad and sit on a bench eating ice cream, or dance in a rainstorm. Either way, she seemed pleased when she saw whatever it was that she saw.

Sarah wondered if we would all get to that point, and she would tell me she knew exactly what moments she would remember when that time came. What highlight reels of her past would surface when she needed them most. So, I thought about that. What moments would be fresh in my mind, when all I had left were my thoughts?

There were so many things that came to mind. Most had occurred when I was a boy, chasing balls in McFarland Field, or opening a fresh pack of baseball cards and finding an Eric Davis rookie. There were times with Grandad when we did nothing but look out dusty windows and relive a time I had never been to, although when he was finished,

I felt I knew. Maybe it would be the trips to town that Grammy and I took, and how we would people watch, and talk about how life needed to slow down for them folks but did not seem to. I liked when Grammy and I would go visit Grandad for our talks. I needed to see him, as much as I needed time with her. Momma. I had very little recollection of who she had been, only who she was now. What if when we are nearing our end, we can go back to anytime we choose, regardless of how deeply buried in our memories it had become? I would go back to a time when Momma and I were swinging on a tire swing in the yard, laughing as I spun around and around, falling off when I was too dizzy to hold on any longer. Then, I would jump up and do it again.

I'd remember the Reds. The night they won the series was great, but it was that first game that meant the most. That night was the start of so much in my life. My family coming together for me, knowing what I needed better than I had. The anticipation of the seven-game series, that only needed four. Who could have known? I'd return to the time Janet and I played the license plate game. Such a small and seemingly unimportant thing, but years later, perhaps my fondest memory of Janet and me.

Whatever it would be, life was full of more remarkable moments than we realize. Most of the seemingly basic moments, became the most important of all. It was becoming apparent that the big moments, while carrying a lot of weight in our memories and hearts and decisions in life, were not necessarily more important than the smaller ones.

As I scanned over what had shaped my life, I realized that the little things mattered more and more. It was picking the flowers, eating the ice cream, talking to someone I could not see any longer. Those moments had left the lasting impact I needed to become the man I wanted to be, and I was able to harness them and share them with others now.

Sarah felt a strong desire to marry as soon as possible, and so we did. Planning the wedding was difficult what with me constantly traveling, zigzagging from state to state across the country. Not only was travel frequent, but speaking to others about grief and pain, helping ensure they could turn their lives onto a positive path, was taxing and my time was sparce. As a result, we had to hurriedly plan for our wedding. It did not matter though. Neither Sarah nor I were interested in lavish affairs. Her mother and father had offered to pay for the wedding Sarah dreamed of as a child, but she changed how she viewed our wedding day many times over the past several years. She wanted simple, yet elegant. Just the closest people to her and me, and when we looked at options for a location, there was only one in her mind.

She wanted Grammy and Momma there, and at that point, there was only one possibility. We were married in the back yard of the home I grew up in, and the home Grammy had been confined to. No one needed to ask why we chose that as the venue for our special day, because they knew. They knew Sarah, and they knew her bond with my family. The day was everything she envisioned, and the most important people we had in our lives, all attended. Janet and Benny were there, with their son Walter, who was just one. Davey, who finally had settled down some, brought his live-in girlfriend Maria with him. She was good for Davey. Loud, but good. We all took to her from the start. Thelma Louise and Mike were there with their brood, and of course, Momma was there.

We made Grammy comfortable enough to come out. Davey fashioned a chair that allowed her to lay back, but still be a part of the wedding. She did not speak, but she motioned and smiled the entire time. She knew. She had to have known what was happening, because I knew her, and I knew that smile. When I kissed her at the very start of the ceremony, she smiled, and I swear I saw her wink. Maybe it had been the sun in her eyes. Maybe it was an involuntary reaction. Whatever it was, I saw it as a wink. My wink.

The scene was ideal. The yard was mowed, just enough to have the grass settle down some, but not down far enough to cut the dandelions throughout its landscape. They peeked out above the grass, surprising bits of bright yellow, and provided the perfect backdrop for our day, for us, and for the moment. And I? I would hold on to that day, for the rest of my life. But more importantly, as Grandad had taught me, I would hold onto day two.

Chapter 22

Going Home

* * *

I was in Vermont, speaking at a convention for Real Estate professionals along with several other, more well-known speakers and professionals from all walks of life and backgrounds. Some were athletes, and some had started businesses out of the trunks of their cars, literally selling whatever product they had, and had turned that into multimillion-dollar empires. There was one woman there who had lost both of her legs just above her knees when an IED exploded while she was serving in Iraq, during the time we had invaded after 9-11. She had been so utterly depressed and had tried taking her life on more than one occasion, and now here she was, speaking out to a mass of thousands of people who were looking at her, at us, for a hint of inspiration to build their careers further. It was one of the largest speaking engagements I had ever been a part of, and I was learning from each speaker. Then, my phone went off.

It was Sarah, and she started by asking how things were

going, which was a normal start to conversation for us. She always liked to know how the people were receiving my message, and what I felt about the particular group I was speaking in front of. I asked her how Grace, our first and only child thus far, was getting along. Was she allowing her mother to sleep at all? I knew Sarah was having trouble with that, but now that things were going well for our business venture, she was able to take time off from work when she needed, and that made a big difference for us all.

"She's good, Ronnie, missing her Daddy," Sarah told me after a pause.

"Sarah, what's wrong? Is everything alright?" I questioned, knowing from the tone of her voice and the slight hesitation she took, that she needed to tell me something.

"Ronnie, Grammy is not well. She's having trouble breathing and her doctor said…Ronnie, can you just come home? I know you are in Vermont, but if you can get back, that would be best, Ronnie."

A lot of my motivational speeches revolved around this simple, now frail woman, who had done so much for me in my life, by just honestly being the woman she was. She was anything but simple, but she hated to be known for anything else. All she ever wanted to be remembered for was a simple country woman, who had lived her life the way God had intended for her to live it. She lived not on her terms, in her mind. She lived on His, with a purpose that only she and He knew. When we look at our lives, sometimes we see what we accomplish disguised as purpose, and it is not always that easy. Purpose isn't about grand accomplishments, or how much money we made over the course of our lives. It's not about motivational speaking or working in a big red brick office building that had once been wide open land filled with flowers and weeds. It is not about wearing a stately tie to impress those who did not.

Purpose was something much greater, yet simpler at the same time. Grammy's purpose was the way she lived and balanced her life, and the life she provided to others whose care she was entrusted with. It was the way she gave life to things around her that no one else thought twice about. She understood, as Grandad had helped her see, that absolutely everything we encountered along life's journey, whether seen with open eyes, or felt with a blind heart, had purpose, and so did she. I knew that I was part of her purpose. Helping me become a man that she, Grandad and Momma could be proud of was just one part of her purpose, and I knew I owed her for sharing all of that with me.

My portion of the speaking engagement had been over for some time, and though there was a meet and greet we did after such events, I knew I had to head home right then. This could possibly be the last time I would get to see Grammy, and while she may not need me, or feel my presence, I needed to be there.

By the time I arrived at Grammy's home, Sarah was sitting by her side with a damp rag on her head, just holding it there, smiling and humming to her. Janet and Thelma Louise were on the opposite side, touching her arm to let her know that she was not alone in her final moments. Davey was standing at the foot of her bed, his hand on his chin, looking as if he would break down at any moment, but was holding it in so that Grammy had this time in peace. All of the McFarlands, except for Momma, were accounted for. There was no way that any of us would not do whatever we could, to be there for what would be the last moments for this amazing, caring, selfless woman we had all come to love, more as a mother than a grandmother. She was one of the three parents we had throughout our lives, and each of us felt the same about that.

When Sarah saw me, she motioned for me to come over, and handed me the lukewarm cloth from her hand. She told me to just press it lightly on Grammy's forehead, as it seemed to comfort her some. I did as I was told. Looking down at her, I leaned in, and talked to her quietly, but I knew everyone still heard the words my heart was singing. Maybe it was just the way people talked when they were saying goodbye.

"Grammy, It's Jasper. I'm here now. We are all here. I probably told you a thousand times how grateful I was for you, but never for the final time, and this is harder on me than I ever imagined it would be. Remember that time we spoke at Grandad's place, and I wondered if he could hear us when we talked during our picnic with him? I learned that the answer was yes, he could hear us. Just like I know, you can hear me now. I love you, Grammy. As a son, as a grandson, as a young man, who has realized that your purpose for us was not a one-time thing, but a lifetime of little gifts of your valuable time and abundant energy. Your lessons and your wonderful, giving heart. How you sacrificed the life you knew, for the life you wanted for all of us. We have that life Grammy, each of us. This room is filled with the product of your sacrifices and without that, we are standing in a very different place. Thank you, for all you have done, and for all you will continue to do throughout our lives. For being you. I love you Grammy. Please, never stop listening to me, and never stop speaking to me. I will need so much more from you, and I know I can count on you. It's time Grammy, it's your time. You can go knowing what you leave behind is a seed of you that you planted with love. I love you Grammy. Until we meet again..."

Davey, starting to cry now, just said to her,

"Grammy, I'm going to give you a swift kick in your ass for doing this to me. I love you. Say hi to Grandad for us. Okay?"

With that, we heard one final drawn out breath of air, her lungs fighting with all they had left, and then nothing. She was no longer what she had been for us. She had moved on, and I hoped Grandad was at the top of the steps, arms stretched out and a wide grin upon his face, ready to give her the grand tour.

Just then, it started to rain outside, and Janet, in true Janet fashion, went over to the door, opened it, and walked out on the front porch without uttering a word. Barefoot, she stepped off the porch, onto the front lawn, and raised her head gently to the sky, allowing the rain to cover her as if it were the warmth of the sun for anyone else. We all laughed, walked to the door, and did the same. Each of us were on the front lawn of the house we had known all our lives, covered in the wet rain that had seemingly come out of nowhere, and we danced. We hugged. We felt. It was as if Grandad had ordered the rain, so that when Grammy arrived, he could take her hand, and run into a theater, drenched, but laughing as he had so many years ago. I just looked up, and said,

"Grandad, she's all yours once again. Thank you, for letting us have her for so long, even though it could never be long enough. Now, dance with her Grandad. She's been waiting for you to ask."

The next morning, we were looking through things in the house, moving old boxes and orange milk crates, trying to find documents we would need, and collecting photographs we would want. Janet had been upstairs going through items in what was once the bedroom she shared with Thelma Louise as a child. When she came downstairs, she had a smile on her face, as if she knew something I did not. She held behind her back something and asked me to guess what she had there.

"Janet, I have no clue," and I laughed, confused.

She pulled her arms to the front, and there in her hands was a beaten brown shoebox, tattered on the ends, and faded, with a small water stain on the top. She handed it to me, and I immediately sat down on the floor where I was standing, laying it on my lap, running my hand across the top slowly, knowing what was in the box. I had forgotten all about the shoebox over the years, with all the things that had gotten in the way of what was once so important to me.

I pulled open the top and looked down on the contents still in there from a few decades ago. It was like opening a door to the past that had long since gone by, but somehow was here as if I were still that eight-year-old boy. Time had refused to slow down, but time had given me a gift regardless. That gift was the ability to revisit my past and memories, whenever I wanted. With just a small box, I was able to go back and remember all those times I spent collecting those cards, and the sheer excitement I felt when Momma would bring me a fresh pack of cards home to open, just because. I remembered Grammy sitting there with me, after Momma had been sick, and laughing as I told her to smell the wrapper, because the wax that held those packs together, had a smell you could simply never forget. I could smell it right now, even though the packs were long gone. That same smell came back because time allowed it to.

I took out first the cards on the very top, and slowly slid them from one hand over to the other, as I had done so many times as a boy. There were dozens of cards with the image of Eric Davis on them, and I remembered how I imagined I was him, swinging for the deep fences, on those wonderful days Davey and his friends allowed me to tag along. There were other players too, of course, but those were the cards I remembered and treasured most. I had not become the pro player that I dreamed of, but that was only because it was not my purpose in life. It was someone else's.

Then when the cards were safely out of the way, I saw a black box that I could not remember the contents of.

When I opened it, there were a pair of tarnished sterling silver round cufflinks. The very ones Grandad handed to me while he was still very much alive. I realized I never did purchase a shirt that accepted cufflinks but knew that was on the top of my to-do list now.

To the left of the box was my green spiral notebook. The one that held all the questions that people told me I would understand when I got older, and here I was. Older. Sarah looked at me, and I just laughed.

"These are all the things I thought I would need answered as a kid, but no one would tell me what those answers were," I said, smiling.

The truth was, I was not even sure of the questions I had put down in my notebook. I showed Janet and asked if she remembered giving it to me, and she nodded that she did. It was because of Janet, I had written down what I pondered as a young boy, and thus, would allow me to take another ride into the past, which I had long since forgotten. I would need to read the notebook later because my curiosity was taking over. I could not wait to see all the things I had needed answers for, and now, maybe, just maybe I could give myself those answers.

The last thing in the box was a folded piece of white lined paper. When I opened it, I knew immediately what it was. It was the letter I tried so hard to address years ago, when we were driving out to see Momma for the first time. That same letter I struggled over while sitting at the dining table, and the same letter I had asked both Davey and Janet how to address.

"What's that, Ronnie?" Sarah asked, curiously.

"This? This, I will tell you about soon. I just need some time."

That shoebox was a treasure to me, and I had forgotten all about it. Janet was just moving around some things when she stumbled on it, wondering if there were papers for Grammy in there. There were things so much more important in that box, and now I had it once again in my hands. I promised I would not forget this plain shoebox ever again.

When I was finished, I placed the lid gently back down, and walked it over to the front door, so I would not forget to take it with me. I needed some things out of it shortly, so it was important to place it where I would remember it when we left.

"Ronnie, one more thing. Can I talk with you, alone for a second?" Janet asked.

This seemed serious, but really with Grammy just passing, it could be anything. We all had a lot going on, and there were so many things to go through that it could be a little overwhelming for each of us. Maybe she just wanted to talk about the final arrangements for the funeral for Grammy. We already knew she would be buried where Grandad was, but we did not know much else about what we had to do. That night we were to meet with the funeral director and make all the arrangements.

"What's up, sis?" I asked her, with a slight smile, trying to read her face.

"Ronnie, before Grammy passed, and before she was

forgetting everything and anything, she sat me down and asked me to do her a big favor when the time came. She handed me an envelope and told me that inside was something meant just for you. That when she passed, she felt you should finally know, Ronnie. So, she wrote that out on what is apparently in this envelope, and now, I am doing what was her last request of me. Handing this to you."

Confused, I looked at the envelope in my hand, and then back at Janet.

"Well, did she tell you what was in it, Janet?"

Janet looked at me, smiled slightly, and told me what Grammy had told her,

"Ronnie, in the envelope, on a plain white index card, is the name of your father. She told me she knew who he was, but she felt that you needed to grow and experience life before you knew who he was. I am not sure of the reasoning, and she did not tell me who he was or elaborate beyond that. She just said that only you could be the one to tell us if you decided to. Those were her complete instructions, so I am just doing what she made me promise I would."

I fell back a few steps and stared at the envelope. I wanted to tear it open and see who this man was that left me alone before I was even born. To see who this man was that had allowed Momma to raise me on her own, and why? Why did he do that to us? Was there a reason he could provide that would make sense, or would it just be an excuse? Maybe a bullshit excuse he had given Momma years ago? All these years of not knowing who he was, and

now, in my hands, was the answer. I held the envelope up to
the sun and tried to see if I could see in without opening it.
I could not. Then, I turned it over, to see just how tightly it
was sealed, and it was sealed much better than those wax
covered card packs were. The only way to see what was
inside the envelope was to tear it open, but I could not
bring myself to do that. Not yet anyway.

"Do the others know, that you had this? Do they know
what is in the envelope, sis?" I asked.

"They only know what I do. That Grammy gave me
this for you, and that she intended for you to open it when
you were ready. They know what is inside, but not who is
inside. She would only say, that this was for you to share,
if you so wished," Janet told me.

"Thanks, sis. I'm going to just go back in and work. I
need to deal with this later."

I needed time. Time to talk with Sarah. Time to think
about what this could mean for me, and the change it might
make over the course of my life. It was not an easy decision
for me, because once I opened the letter, and looked at
the index card tucked inside, there was no turning back.
I needed to be ready for what was coming, and this was
not the right time. Not now. I needed time to deal with
losing Grammy, and that would come first. She had not
abandoned me, so she took precedence over everything else.
Especially over the name in that envelope, some stranger
who had decided long ago not to know me and all I was.

When I walked back inside with Janet, everyone was
looking up at me, to see my reaction. I just put my head

down slightly, then looked at them all and smiled. Placing the letter in my back pocket, I told them I would open it when the time was better. Davey stood up, came over to me, and hugged me.

"Squirt, I love you, brother. Whatever is on that card, and whatever anyone ever tells you, we are not half-brothers. You were and will always be my brother, period. None of this half stuff. Okay? You do what you need to do, and if you need me to go and give that guy, whoever he is, a swift kick in the ass, you know you can always count on me," he said with a smile.

Chapter 23

Saying Goodbye

* * *

Ⅰt is hard to explain how it looks, when an entire town comes out, with all their children, and their grandchildren, to say goodbye to someone most knew, and others had only heard about. It appeared that over a short ninety years, this humble, modest woman, who had touched each one of the McFarland children endlessly, had also touched countless other folks clear across town. Some of the faces were familiar, including the old man and his wife that had operated the ice cream shop we had visited an untold number of times over the years. There was her hairdresser April, who was the only person in town she would allow to do a cut and color of her hair. Even when Grammy was forced to remain in home, April would stop by and give her a trim. She just felt it was the least she could do, and prior to Grammy getting stricken and confined to her bed, she never missed an appointment.

People from all walks of life, young and old, were lined up and down the center aisle, and out the front door of the old church. Most were smiling, though some were crying. We honestly did not expect this sort of gathering, and we all looked at each other in utter amazement. The priest, who would be performing the mass, had pulled me aside, and told me that if there ever was a measure in life of how one person could make an impact, we were witnessing it here and now. I had to agree. When we are alive, we never get to see this amount of people congregating in one place, not even at a wedding. It was enough for me to understand that although I had loved my grammy, and she had made an impact on my life like no one else, she still had plenty enough left in her to give to others.

We were standing at the front of the church, to the right of where Grammy was laying, peacefully, in her favorite teal blue dress with yellow flowers along the sleeves. Janet had insisted we stand to the right side of her over the left. It was her way of giving this day to Grammy alone. Her anxiety would not affect her. Not today, not here, not now.

Momma was standing next to Davey, and we sat a chair behind her so she could sit as she needed. She looked around confused, but it was as if she knew she needed to be there and needed to be at the front of the gathering, even if she did not quite understand why. Thelma Louise made that decision. At first, we felt it better and safest for Momma to just sit in one of the pews along with a nurse we would bring along to be with her. But Thelma Louise reasoned that when Momma one day regained more of herself back she should not have more regrets than the years she had already lost to her illness. Being with her family, at her own momma's funeral was something she would have wanted to do and Thelma Louise insisted we help make that happen for Momma. We agreed. It made sense like none of us had expected.

As the service started, a man at the front of the church said a few words.

"Thank you all for gathering here today to pay your final respects to Mildred Elizabeth Hale McFarland. The family would like you to know how much they appreciate each and every one of you for coming out, and that they believe their grandmother is watching over us all from above and smiling down. Please come up and greet the family as you walk by and say goodbye. At the conclusion of the service, if anyone would like to speak, the family asks that you come up and let me know, and I will add you to the list. Thank you."

He motioned for the first person in line to come on up and start what would be the last time any of these people would see this amazing woman. It finally hit me. This was going to also be the last time I would see her, and I felt this overwhelming feeling of both guilt and sadness fall over me. Guilt because I wish I had been back for more than just the final hours of her life. I knew she was not doing great and should have stayed and spent whatever time I could with her. I wondered to myself; did she know I was not there until the end? If she did, how did she feel about it? She knew I was busy with my speaking and making a name for myself, but did she understand, and was she okay with it? Janet, who was standing next to me, grabbed my arm as if she knew what was going through my head and whispered to me,

"Ronnie, she's okay with it all. She had a fantastic ride, and this is a sendoff she could only dream of. It's okay, little brother. She was proud of you."

I smiled, knowing she was probably right. I mean, I had known this woman all my life, and could have still never expected all of this, even though I knew she was loved. She was just so damn special.

As the people came up, they mostly knelt by Grammy, said a few final words, and walked over to us, hands extended. Several hugged each of us and thanked us for sharing her and all she was, with them. One by one, they walked by, and paid their respects. The line did not seem to grow any shorter, and Davey whispered at one point,

"If she makes me miss the game tonight, I'm going to give her a swift kick in the ass."

We all laughed, and Janet told us to stop, but she was laughing too. It was an ice-breaking moment we needed desperately because we were all mentally and physically exhausted. The day was long, and I still had to speak, as the family asked me to on behalf of all of us. Speaking was natural and easy for me, but I wanted to get this one right. It was a moment I had thought about for many years, and here it was in front of me.

When the line finished, after what seemed like hours upon hours, and I felt as if a thousand people had touched my hands and offered their condolences, it was time for the mass. We figured most of the folks would pay their final respects and be on their way to whatever they had planned that day, but very few left. They were still standing there as the mass started. The priest began the mass and asked an altar boy to bring over the microphone so the people at the back and gathered out front on the steps, could hear what he was saying.

As the mass ended, he blessed Grammy and walked back up to the podium.

"At this time, we have some people who would like to say a few words about Mildred, or Millie as some of you remember her. Please come forward, and then we will turn this over to her grandson, Ronnie, who has prepared a few words as well on behalf of the family."

People walked up, and while we knew most of them, there were a few we did not. They told stories of running into Grammy in town and getting to know her as she stopped in their shops. Stories of how she babysat some of them as young children and allowed them to eat an extra sweet treat if they promised not to tell their parents. People chuckled when one woman told that story. A man, who I never set eyes on, seemed to remember both Grammy and Grandad for a long time. His message was short. He had only wanted to let everyone know that he was happy they were finally back together, and to thank us all for sharing our Grammy with him. We smiled at each other, but no one knew who he was. He left out the door as he finished. Tears in his eyes, and a look of sadness on his face.

Then, after the final person spoke, it was my turn. I had spoken in front of thousands of people, and it never bothered me much. It was what I did best. But here, I was feeling a bout of anxiety. My mind was racing, wanting so badly to make the right impression on this crowd of people and do my grammy the justice she greatly deserved.

As I reached the podium, I cleared my throat some, and placed the papers I had in my hand, on to the desk before me. Then, I looked over to where my brother and sisters and family were seated. I looked at each of their faces and smiled. Sarah was seated with them naturally, and her parents too. Benny was seated with Janet, as was Mike with Thelma Louise. Maria, whom Davey had fallen head over heels for by now, was holding his hand. All those eyes out before me throughout the church, seemed to send me a calming relief I did not expect.

"My name is Ronnie Jefferson McFarland Jr. Today, though, my name is Jasper," I began.

"We are here to celebrate not the death, but rather the life of Mildred, whom I only knew as Grammy. She was, to me and my siblings, the most amazing person we had been blessed with, and if you had the chance to speak with her, even if only for a minute or two, you can understand why we felt that way. Imagine having a lifetime with her. I am truly blessed for that time and feel a little selfish that I was able to have that much of this remarkable human.

Aside from the traditional thank you's that people say at these types of gatherings, I want to read you a letter. A letter I wrote some twenty plus years ago and found recently at my grammy's home. Please bear with me."

I took a letter off the table in front of me and unfolded

it. Before I began, I looked over to where my grammy was lying, and smiled at her,

"I have no idea how I am supposed to address this. I could go with dear Ronnie. I could be more formal and start it with dear Ronnie Jefferson McFarland Jr, but that doesn't sound right. I could also just say Dear Jasper, because Grammy likes that name for me, and I kind of like it too. It is the nickname she gave me and none of the other kids have a nickname like mine.

But this letter today is about my momma, and she called me Ronnie, so that is how I will address it.

So here it goes,

Dear Ronnie. I hope you are well. I hope you are all grown up, and that you are playing right field for the Cincinnati Reds. If you are playing left field, I will not be upset either, but just make sure you are an outfielder, OK? I also hope you are not wearing a tie. Or a suit for that matter."

The people in the church started to smile and chuckle, looking at me in my fitted suit and my bright blue tie I had neatly tied around my neck. I shrugged and smiled as I continued.

"Remember, we do not want to wear a suit because they do not fit well, and the ties rub against our necks, and make them red with a rash. So, I know you will not be wearing those.

Well, today is not a good day. Momma is in a place far away from here, and I am not sure how to feel about that. I remember when Grandad died, we did not get to see him again, but Grammy told me he was still watching us, so that was not all bad. But this is different. This is my momma, and well, while it is good she will be back one day, I am sure going to miss her until she is. I really want to talk with her and tell her I am proud of her. That she is a good momma, and that I want to talk with her a lot more. It does not seem fair to me. Why did God need to do this to my momma? Maybe he does not know that I need her more. Maybe I was not praying enough. Ok, I was not praying at all, really, but now I promise to pray more. I will."

There was complete silence in the room now, as I continued on with the letter I had written so many years before, as that eight-year-old boy,

"I want to write to you, so that we remember Momma as she was. She is kind, pretty, and works hard. She always brings me baseball cards when I am good, and even sometimes when I am not so good. The last time she bought me a pack, I got two Eric Davis cards, and told her how lucky that pack was. She just smiled at me and said, "Oh yea, Ronnie? How about that! You must have a lot of luck on your side." She was right. I had a lot of luck, until today. So, Grammy will need me to step up more. Last year she lost Grandad, and now, she doesn't have Momma to help out. Grammy is also hard-working, and she did all she could to help Momma while she was sick. I saw Grammy come home from the hospital sad when they told her Momma was needing to go to a place to get more help. She tried hard to hide it, but I could tell. She looks thinner lately. She looks a little older. I hope she is OK. I will pray more from now on, so God does not take Grammy from me. That he will not take Thelma Louise, Janet, or Davey from me. I know Davey and I do not get along, but he is my brother, and the truth is, I need him. With Momma gone, I need everyone.

So, God, if you are reading this, please first say hi to my grandad. He was a good grandad, and I miss him a lot. Next, please make sure my momma comes home to us, fixed. Grandad told me a long time ago, that God sometimes took Momma's because he needed them for all the little kids that died. I know she's a great pick, but please, God, leave her here with us. Then, can you please protect my grammy? Grammy is so much more than just a regular grammy. She has been like a mom to me. Like a dad. She has filled so many spots in my life when I needed someone. She never complains to me. She never cries. She just does what it is she does, but God, can you please leave her here for me? For Thelma Louise, for Janet...even for Davey? Can you? I will promise you, I will be good. From here on out, I will be good.

Thank you. And Ronnie, Jasper? I hope we did all right. Even if we aren't playing for the Reds. I hope whatever we are doing, we are doing it right, and not wearing a suit. Or a tie. Because that would be just stupid.

Thanks,

Ronnie Jefferson McFarland Jr, also known as Jasper, to Grammy."

I then looked down, and as much as I tried not to, I felt warm tears coming down from the corners of my eyes. As

I looked up over to my family, they too, were crying. Even Davey. Momma was just looking down, and I do not think she understood, but I wish she had.

"For those wondering, I never made it as a right fielder for the Reds. Nor did I play left field. The suit and tie, well, let's just let that one go."

People just laughed.

"I am wearing a special pair of cufflinks for the very first time. Ones my grandad gave to me many years ago, and I had long forgotten about. Not anymore. I will wear these for a long time to come," I continued.

"As for the letter. It does not begin to describe what this woman meant to us, but it shows a start to what she would take on, without a single complaint.

All I hope is that when she reached those gates, Grandad was standing tall there, waiting with a smile and an extended arm. Taking her by the hand, and leading her into heaven, so they can once again, be together to create a new set of memories, or relive the ones they had already had."

I looked over once again to where my grammy was and I smiled.

"Grammy. You have no idea of the impact you had on my life. On our lives. Just know, without you, none of us are the people standing here now," and I winked at her.

"The final thing I wish to tell you all is this. Go. Go and sit with those that have gone before you. Talk with them and ask them questions. I know this may sound strange but trust me. They know you are there. They do. They need us to visit with them. They miss us as much as we miss them. So, be sure to go, and say hi from time to time. Have a picnic. Bring wildflowers and pour them a glass of lemonade. Just be there."

As I walked by her on my way back to where my family was seated, I laid a simple white envelope next to Grammy in the casket. Then, I returned to my family, who were all standing and waiting for me, and we hugged. We just hugged.

Chapter 24

About That Envelope

* * *

Time went ahead the way time does, and life took on a new normal. We took Grammy's house and gutted it over the next several months, so that we could turn it into a home Momma could return to. We were all doing well, and despite what the hospitals advised, we decided it was time to bring her home. She needed to spend her time in a place that was closer to us and a little more familiar, so that she could hopefully someday, regain a little of what she had sadly lost.

Everything looked great, and we all had a hand in that. After a few months, Momma was in place and had round the clock care. We handpicked nurses and allowed Sarah to oversee Momma's care. She knew what to look for, and we had complete trust in her. It was so nice being that close to Momma again, and yet it still felt so far. All I wanted was for her to notice me, one more time.

I continued my weekly visits to where Grandad and now Grammy were, even though they were mostly not on Saturdays any longer. My Saturdays were filled with travel, so I could try and be home more during the week with Sarah and our growing family. I still found time to go and talk to them though, and they still talked back each time. Something new I noticed on my trips there, was there seemed to be a rising number of people stopping to visit with their loved ones. I even saw that mother, now older and a little frail herself, visiting with her daughter. That made me smile to see her, and although I wanted to go over and talk with her, I felt it better to leave her be, spending that time there listening to her child.

Lost in all this was the envelope I had placed beside Grammy. Davey asked me one night as we all sat around having a beer after working on the house for Momma, something that had entirely slipped his mind.

"Ronnie, whoa. I never asked you about the card Grammy gave you. You know, the one with your dad. Whatever happened to that? Did you ever open it, or are you still unsure?"

I smiled at him, without looking over. Took a long sip of my beer and told him what I had done.

"Big brother, do you remember at Grammy's funeral, when I was finished with my speech, and I walked by her casket, looked in, and dropped a letter to her? Do you remember that part?" I asked.

"Noooo, you did not. You did not put that in with her. Tell me you did not. Ronnie, you did, didn't you?"

I just look over at him, winked and said, "Davey, I have all the family I ever needed. I do not need anymore.

Whoever my dad was, decided I was not worth his time, and the truth is, he is not worth mine. I thought about it for a few long nights, and realized, I did not need to know any more than I did. We are family, big brother. I'm good with that. I'm good."

Davey smirked, and sat back, laughing out loud. He was proud of me for having the ability to pass on knowing what I had wondered about for many years. I had grown enough to realize, I did not need know who my father was and it felt good. I was lucky enough to have a wonderful, supportive family, and having more, did not mean having better. The name on that paper? It was just a name, and that was it. Not a person I would talk to as we ate ice cream and people watched together. Or a person I would ask questions to and learn from. It was a meaningless name, and so I left it with Grammy, knowing she may have been the only person other than Momma to know. And I was just fine with that.

It was safe to say, we were happy with how we were raised, and proud of how we had turned out. Having a momma like we had, who sacrificed to the point it changed her forever, in turn, changed us forever. We refused to allow her illness and our losses to define us, instead we allowed those things to help shape us. When Grammy stepped up as she did, she somehow made it seem seamless, and that was no small feat. How she knew what we would need, always impressed me. She knew when to push us, and when to let us learn the hard way. She knew what questions to answer, and which ones to let us answer for ourselves. She had the ability to lead the way and let us follow along, allowing us each to go at our own pace, and with our own sized steps. If we stumbled, she told us how to dust ourselves off and stand back up on our own, and that was a lesson that served us well through our lives. She taught us tenacity and independence, but when we really needed her, she was always right there to teach or, if need be, to carry us through whatever challenges we faced.

Grandad, that man teaches me still to this day. Every time I see a weed, some insignificant moss growing where someone would prefer it not, or a simple dandelion growing out of a small crack in the sidewalk, I stop to think of him, and I wonder, what was its purpose. Then I would catch myself, and realize, I did not need to understand its purpose. It did not depend on me knowing.

Every once in a while, I drove Grandad's old Chevy truck into town, just to look at the familiar scenery, but from his vantage point. I never washed the windows because that was the way he saw his world. Dusty, dirty at times, but in his opinion, it was perfect just the way it was.

Janet told me once, that Grammy explained to her the special reason for the name she had given me, but with all that was going on, and how much we had to do at the end of her life, she had forgotten to tell me. It was funny really, how Jasper came about. There is a place called Jasper, in Alberta Canada, and it was where Grandad and Grammy had gone for their honeymoon. Grammy, on her return, swore it was heaven on earth. They had such a love for that place but sadly had never been able to return. When she saw me for the first time, her fondest memory came flooding back to her. She felt like calling me Jasper brought a small piece of that place home for her. She wanted me to carry a name that made her think of heaven on earth, and so to her Jasper was my name.

One ordinary evening, while visiting with Momma, along with Sarah and our children, my oldest asked me why Grammy called me Jasper. As I told the story, Momma laughed, and spoke with a voice I had not heard since I was eight years old. It was hard to tell what she was saying if you did not know, but I could tell. I knew in an instance, that she had found a small part of her voice. She struggled, but she got those few words out.

"Jasper." She smiled, "Momma's boy."

Momma was finally home.

The End

The License Plate Game

Pennsylvania

Wisconsin

Vermont

Ohio

Tennessee

Virginia

Maryland

Illinois

Texas

Montana

Janet McFarland

Made in the USA
Monee, IL
29 September 2023

43655926R00173